You've Got to Hear This

Untold Stories of Jazz Musicians

James A. Vedda

Copyright © 2022 James A. Vedda
All rights reserved.

Dedication

To Lin, my wife and best friend.

Other books by James A. Vedda:

Choice, Not Fate: Shaping a Sustainable Future in the Space Age (2009)

Becoming Spacefarers: Rescuing America's Space Program (2012)

Table of Contents

Introduction ix

Marshall Hawkins: Making music on land and at sea 1
    When bands went to sea 3
    Hawk goes to school 9
    Assignment at sea 13
    Hawk goes ashore 19
    Back to sea 23
    Teaching and directing the Navy's finest musicians 25
    Tightening up on testing 30
    Directing ensembles again 32
    Celebrity encounters 33
    A musician's work is never done 35
    References 36

The Ubiquitous Marvin Stamm 37
    From the home of the blues to a Texas training ground 39
    Have trumpet, will travel 41
    New connections, new opportunities 43
    Don't get too comfortable 47
    Back to the Big Apple 48
    Live from the studios 52
    On the road again 57
    That's not all, folks! 61
    Discography 63

Holly Hofmann: Shaping the Identity of Jazz Flute 65
    Early (legendary) mentors 68

    Westward migration – Colorado to California 69
    Collaborations 71
    Preserving San Diego's jazz culture 75
    Shaping young (and not-so-young) minds 78
    What's this? A female flutist from the San Diego? 79
    References 82
    Discography 82

Joe Eckert: To the Air Force and Beyond 84
    From academia to military life 86
    Basic training for an "old" musician 89
    Performances and tours 90
    Performing abroad 95
    Maintaining support for military bands 98
    Life outside The Note 102
    The next chapter 107
    References 107
    Discography 108

Encounters with Jazz Influencers 110
    Lessons from "The Old Man" 112
    On the road – sort of 114
    Everybody's favorite band director 116
    Shaping the future 121
    Reference 122
    Discography 122

Jazz Futures 123
    Perceptions of jazz 123
    More than just the backup band 127
    World music 131
    Jazz jocks 132

Cool curricula... *134*
A coming resurgence? *136*
References... *136*
About the author **138**

Introduction

This project started a few years ago when I discovered that my friend Marshall Hawkins, who had a long, productive, eventful music career starting in the U.S. Navy, had no written chronicle of his experiences. It was clear that his story needed to be told, so we started to explore it together in a series of interviews. The result is the first chapter of this book.

The research and writing process made me wonder how many other interesting stories remained untold among musicians I know. Many musicians are good storytellers but are not necessarily inclined to express themselves in written prose. And some are just too darn modest. I decided to seek out other jazz performers and teachers who influenced me and countless others.

This book focuses on a handful of artists who have enriched my jazz evolution in some way, and who were willing to have their stories published. It is not intended to comprehensively chronicle these musicians' lives, nor is it a statistically significant random sample of jazz artists. These stories are here because they are interesting and entertaining and have been lived by people who are among the unsung heroes of jazz. (Or at least, the not-sufficiently-sung heroes.)

In addition to their performances, recordings, and teaching, many prolific musicians have given us stories that are inspiring or tragic or funny or poignant, or are simply great yarns about noteworthy experiences. Biographers are happy to tell the stories of artists who have achieved legendary status and are enshrined in some jazz hall of fame, and the artists' fans are eager to read about everything from big career-altering events to little-known behind-the-scenes anecdotes. But you don't need to have a name as recognizable as Duke Ellington or Tony Bennett to have interesting tales to tell – about successful (or embarrassing) performances, about working with inspirational artists, or about personal and societal challenges along the way. Most of the time, these entertaining and instructive tales get heard only by fellow musicians during breaks at a gig or rehearsal, or at a post-performance late-night meal. This book is an attempt to give voice to a few of my favorite musicians and introduce them to a wider audience that can enjoy and learn from their exploits.

The stories in these chapters span the 1940s to the present. The dynamic evolution of the U.S. music market during this period saw the ups and downs of many musical styles. Jazz has been present throughout, demonstrating resilience and ongoing appeal even in the absence of commercial success on a par with other genres. Experiences in the jazz community also have been reflective of developments throughout American society, such as fluctuations in the U.S. economy, racial tensions, the increasing strength of women in the workforce, and the setbacks of the coronavirus pandemic. Readers need not have an affinity for jazz to appreciate what these artists have gone through in pursuit of their passion.

The great keyboard artist Herbie Hancock once observed that contemporary popular music has become more about who's delivering the music than it is about the music itself. Audiences and fans seem to be fixated primarily on the celebrity glamor. This is not a strong factor in jazz, and that is the main reason why, according to Herbie, jazz doesn't enjoy the same level of popularity as other genres. But keeping the focus on the music is a feature, not a bug. I've frequently heard my fellow musicians, including some interviewed for this book, say that "It's all about the music." The look in their eyes says that they mean it. The music they perform and write demonstrates their sincerity. You've got to hear the rest of their stories.

I would like to thank the musicians featured in the following chapters for agreeing to participate in this project, granting me multiple interviews, and reviewing my work to make sure I got it right. If I didn't, it's not their fault.

If you're not already familiar with some of these musicians, I'm proud to be introducing to you (in order of appearance) Marshall Hawkins, Marvin Stamm, Holly Hofmann, Joe Eckert, Jim Anastasi (who passed away before I could interview him), and Gary Langford.

In addition to thanking these artists for their help on the book, I would also like to thank each of them for their body of work and their efforts as teachers. Through their direct or indirect influence, I've been inspired to be a better musician, even as I spent my career in a field unrelated to music. We should all thank them, because they made jazz music better and more enduring.

Jim Vedda
June 2022

Chapter 1

Marshall Hawkins:
Making music on land and at sea

In 2012, I joined the sax section of a Thursday night rehearsal band in the northern Virginia suburbs of Washington, DC. Many of the other players were new to me, and one in particular stood out. Everyone seemed to know and respect the older gentleman playing bass trombone, and some of them called him Hawk. People tended to gather around him to hear his stories, so of course I joined in. The first thing I learned was his name – Marshall Hawkins – and that he had been the first director of the U.S. Navy Commodores jazz ensemble when it was formed in 1969.[*] Very cool – but as I learned, there's a lot more to his story.

A performer on lower brass and string bass, and an ensemble director and arranger, Marshall had a remarkable 22-year career in Navy music that in many ways set the stage for the Navy musicians who followed. According to Hawk's biography on the Navy Band's website, there was a time when 80 percent of the Navy's Bandmasters were his former students because one of his assignments

---

[*] Not be confused with the other Marshall Hawkins (no relation), a jazz bassist who worked with many noted artists (such as Miles Davis and Herbie Hancock) and also grew up in the Washington, DC area.

was to direct the student bandleader course. This was made possible by his promotion in 1957 to Chief Musician (equivalent to Chief Petty Officer), making him eligible to teach at the Navy School of Music and to direct bands, and also making him the first African-American to achieve this position in the post-World War II integrated Navy.

Marshall Hawkins speaking at the 40th anniversary concert of the U.S. Navy Commodores jazz ensemble (Photo credit: U.S. Navy Band, 2009)

The U.S. Navy became racially integrated in 1948 as a result of an executive order from President Harry Truman, and Marshall joined up within a year. He was in the first integrated class of musicians at the Navy School of Music, eventually became one of the school's instructors, and led many ensembles such as the Ceremonial Band, the NATO Band (stationed in Naples, Italy), several small groups, and the aforementioned Commodores jazz ensemble. All of these accomplishments are best appreciated in the context of the time: an era of post-war integration when live music performances were among the most important morale-boosters for deployed sailors.

When bands went to sea

For many years in the mid-20th century, there were two primary means of bringing entertainment to crews at sea: the reels of Hollywood movies carried aboard ship, and the music provided by the onboard bands. Unlike today, there were no pocket-size personal music players, tablets with high-resolution screens, or satellite broadband Internet connections. No real-time links to news, sports, or other diversions from the daily grind of shipboard duties. If it wasn't loaded onto the ship before departure, it wasn't available. Onboard movie selections were very limited and couldn't offer much variety. In the years before Navy ships were transformed by the miracles of modern global telecommunications, even the best Hollywood movies could get a little stale after their umpteenth viewing. And there were no options for direct contact with family and friends back home.

Live music provided by comrades in arms made a big difference. Popular tunes, light classics, and dance music brought memories of home, an escape from the mundane, and national pride inspired by the professionalism of the musicians. Although bands are no longer routinely deployed on ships the way they used to be, similar benefits accrue today. Bands put a public face on the military, support recruiting efforts, and make trips to conflict zones to boost morale and instill pride, just like before.

A proper telling of Marshall's story requires some background on the organization at the heart of it: the Navy School of Music, which was established a few years prior to World War II.

In 1935, U.S. Navy Band director Lt. Charles Benter and other interested leaders recognized the need for a formal music education program. The Navy was growing and the bands serving aboard ships and at naval bases needed to be held to a higher standard. The ceremonial Navy Band in Washington typically got its musicians directly from civilian life, usually from music conservatories. However, the bands serving on the Navy's ships were not so fortunate. They were all pickup bands, grabbing whatever players were available, regardless of their level of proficiency. These musicians primarily came in through a rather informal process that was referred to as the "E-flat school" that had no organization and no music library. The Navy had a large presence in San Diego, as it still does today, and players congregated there. If a ship came into port and needed a trumpet player, for example, the word was passed around and if a trumpeter was available, he could be assigned to the ship. Officially, the responsibility of a military service is to organize, train, and equip, but little of that was happening in Navy music at that time.

Lt. Benter chose James Thurman, a French horn player, to start the Navy School of Music, which set up shop near the 8th Street Gate in the Navy Yard in Washington, DC. Its original building had been used for the milling and storage of flour. In 1940, the school moved across the river to the Navy receiving station and in 1942 became a separate entity from the Navy Band. Prior to this time, the instructors had been members of the Navy Band who got the teaching assignment as additional duty. In the time-honored tradition of multi-tasking, they still had to maintain their usual schedule of rehearsals and performances with the Navy Band, and somehow find the time to go to the Navy School to teach and to direct ensembles. Establishing a dedicated teaching staff rectified this sub-optimal situation and was a big step forward for the school.

Seamen entering the school would be assigned to a sequentially numbered band, and typically would stay with that group throughout their training. In addition to instruction on their individual instruments, they would take classes in music theory, harmony, and ear training, and would have daily ensemble rehearsals. The program was designed to be completed in two years, but could be interrupted at any time if a band was needed to go on a cruise. Many musicians were glad to temporarily suspend the regimen because most of what they did aboard ship was dance band playing, which they enjoyed. At the time, the school had no dance bands – Jim Thurman wouldn't allow that. The school's program included strictly ceremonial or "legit" ensembles. It was a refreshing break when there was an opportunity to play dance music for official functions, such as the annual press ball attended by President Franklin D. Roosevelt.

Although dance bands were deliberately excluded from the curriculum, the dance band repertoire had to come from somewhere. The enterprising bandsmen developed methods to get what they needed. Sometimes, arrangements were copied off of records, a tedious and time-consuming process. When the Navy players had the opportunity to attend performances of the big name bands, like Benny Goodman or Tommy Dorsey, they would ask to borrow the scores for some of their arrangements, and frantically copy them by hand while the show was going on. (Sorry, no copy machines or digital scanners were available in those days.) These methods became less frequent as the so-called "stock" arrangements became widely available.

Stock arrangements were copies of the arrangements used in recordings by the popular big bands, although they were usually altered in ways that would make them easier to perform for local groups around the country that wanted to duplicated the sounds of the famous bands. In addition to the famous bands' arrangements, the stocks included hundreds of tunes that could be used to fill the dance books of local groups. Most of these followed familiar patterns, such as a four-bar introduction, a chorus featuring the brass section playing the lead, a chorus of saxophones in the lead, and then a key change to a final chorus with the full ensemble. Solos were rare in these formulaic dance charts, and when they did occur they usually consisted of just four to eight bars of written melody. This was not the type of material that the Navy players would have found particularly challenging or enjoyable. Fortunately, they had another source.

The players themselves wrote dance arrangements. Many had dance band experience before joining the Navy, so they knew the style, they knew what was popular, and they wrote the kinds of things that they'd like to play. Some were original treatments of well-known songs, and some were derived from recordings. So the individual musicians, especially the chiefs, had their own dance libraries, but the school didn't. This began to change after the war ended. By the time Marshall Hawkins entered the school in 1949, dance bands were active despite the fact that Jim Thurman was still there. (He retired that year and went home to Pennsylvania to teach.)

Sometimes, the cruises that needed bands involved junkets by high officials, such as the time President Roosevelt went on a six-week fishing trip to the Caribbean, followed immediately by a similar (though shorter) trip by the Secretary of the Navy. The school also put together a 28-piece ensemble, sporting brand new uniforms, to perform at the 1939 New York World's Fair, playing honors for officials from all over the world. On the fair's Pan-American Day, the ensemble played the national anthems of 23 countries on live television, which was quite a novelty at that time. Hardly anybody had television sets, so the main viewership was at the TVs set up in the windows of Macy's department store in New York.

The more common experiences were shakedown cruises for ships — their first time out with a full crew — that would go to places like the Caribbean. When the cruise was over, the band members would return to the school and go back to their classes. By the time a two-year program of study was completed, it could take much longer because the shipboard deployments could last many months.

The Navy band program was at its peak enrollment during World War II with 6,800 musicians serving in approximately 285 bands based on ships and on shore. The musicians were not pampered entertainers who sat around waiting for the curtain to go up. They were sailors. They all had non-musical duties to perform, especially when a ship went to battle stations. Often that meant helping the medical unit as stretcher bearers or in some other capacity. But there were other higher-risk assignments, such as the one given to the band aboard the U.S.S. Arizona at Pearl Harbor in 1941. When the Japanese attacked on December 7, all of the band members reported to munitions storage, where they were responsible for transferring ammunition to the topside guns. When that part of the ship took a direct hit, the entire band was killed in an instant.

Hawk was just a kid at the time, but later learned to appreciate the events of that day – the tragic loss, the heroism, the patriotic determination to survive and fight another day – from long friendships with Navy musicians who were survivors of the Pearl Harbor attack.

After the war ended, some of the returning musicians were reassigned to the school, but not all of them were happy about it. They felt it was too academic in its approach and too traditional in its style, and they felt they'd moved beyond that stage as performers. They also resented Jim Thurman's strict discipline. One particularly annoying practice was that Thurman had installed microphones in all of the practice rooms and rehearsal halls so he could monitor from his desk what was going on. (Electronic monitoring of workers by their boss is a practice that started long before the Internet age.) Part of the reason for this, it was believed, was that he wanted to catch anyone who made disparaging remarks about the school or the Navy music program. After experiencing the war, the returning musicians didn't appreciate being treated this way.

Hawk goes to school

Marshall first learned about the Navy music program in 1949 while he was attending Howard University in Washington, DC. The Korean conflict was looming on the horizon, and Hawk expected to be drafted. He discussed his prospects with the university's band director, Bernard Mason, who assured him that the military bands provided good training and experience, and would be a fine start to whatever career path he decided to pursue. Armed with that knowledge, he went to the Navy recruiting office on Constitution Avenue and signed on to be a Navy musician. He passed the initial audition, which required a score of 2.9 or better on a 4.0 scale to pass. He learned later that the passing score varied if the Navy needed more musicians, in which case it could be as low as 2.6.

Before joining the music program, there were eight weeks of recruit training at Great Lakes, Illinois, near Chicago. All types of recruits were trained there, and all went through the same basic program. Fortunately, there were musical ensembles at the training center, allowing Hawk to keep his chops in shape: a drum and bugle corps (in which he played baritone bugle) and a dance band (trombone). But that was just a brief episode on the way to the real Navy music program.

Upon arriving at the Navy School of Music, Marshall was placed in a temporary position until he was assigned to a band. New recruits in that position served as the janitorial staff, which included the Navy's best-known unglamorous duty, swabbing the deck. Even though they weren't on a ship, Navy jargon was in full play. The floor is the "deck," the walls are the "bulkhead," the door is the "hatch," and of course, the lavatory is the "head."

Once assigned to a band, the musicians did all of their scheduled activities as a unit. Each morning, they marched together to the mess hall for breakfast. (Meals were served on less-than-elegant metal trays, just like aboard ship.) After breakfast, they marched to the school to start the day's routine of classes and rehearsals. The process repeated for lunch and for evening chow, so the group had plenty of quality time together.

The musical repertoire was very broad – more than just military marches, although there were plenty of those. The bands worked on light (and sometimes not-so-light) classical pieces and other material similar to what you'd expect to hear from a concert band today. By this time there were a lot of dance gigs, so dance charts for the usual big band instrumentation were part of the routine.

After dinner, some members often had duty, such as standing watches. For those who didn't have duty, it was a good time for individual practice, and most people played at least two instruments. Individual instruction included assigned pieces to practice for the next lesson, just like the music lessons many people remember from childhood. The instructor gave students a practice card indicating how many hours of practice he expected each week. Marshall's family lived in DC, but he "tended to stay on base and practice like crazy. I wanted to have cast iron chops that would never get tired. If I wasn't practicing alone, I would be jamming with some of the other guys. On more nights than I can count, they had to kick us out of the school so they could shut the place down."

If all lessons were confidently prepared and free time remained, some form of entertainment off the base – "going on liberty" – was a popular option. This often occurred on Friday afternoons, but not before a required trip to the rehearsal hall to listen to Rocks & Shoals, the Navy's justice code that was in place prior to the Uniform Code of Military Justice. Friday afternoon liberty could not begin until the seamen sat through a session in which someone read them all the things they could and couldn't do as a member of the military. According to Marshall, "It took all of our training and stamina to keep us awake through this. Those who did not succeed would get whacked in the head to reestablish the required state of consciousness."

The usual routine sometimes changed to accommodate special events. If there was a ceremony of some kind in downtown DC, or a funeral at Arlington National Cemetery, or a combo gig at the officers club, one of the school's ensembles would prepare some appropriate material and get into uniform for the performance. The U.S. Navy Band formerly had handled much of this duty, especially funerals, but handed it off to the school ensembles, which were quite capable of properly representing the Navy. In the early days, these impeccably dressed ensembles would ride to Arlington Cemetery standing in the back of a truck.

When the Navy deployed bands, their size depended on the type of ship or the stature of the installation where they were based. Thirteen-piece "orchestras" went to heavy cruisers, 17-piece bands were on battleships and carriers, and 23-piece bands were placed under the flag officers. (At the school, bandsmen had experience playing in groups as large as 60 pieces.) The 13-piece groups were unusual in that they had two violin players who doubled on another instrument when playing marches or other music without string parts. Often the double was French horn, a seemingly unlikely choice for string players – assuming they were given a choice. The 23-piece bands were a visible component of an admiral's prestige, and in those days the admirals usually took their bands with them when they changed commands.

Hawk was at the school for 18 months before he got assigned to a shipboard ensemble, Band 171. (The Navy was still building bands for shipboard duty using the sequential numbering system that began in 1935.) The 6th Fleet in the Mediterranean was scheduled to get a 23-piece flag band in 1950. Band 171 was in line for that spot, but Hawk got bumped to Band 172 because the school decided to put a higher-ranked euphonium player ahead of him. His new director was a tall, thin, very relaxed character named Nathan Flippin, who of course was nicknamed Flip. Hawk took on additional duties as the band's librarian. (Eventually, he reunited with some of his old Band 171 mates as he made his way through the Mediterranean on another ship.)

Assignment at sea

Band 172 arrived in New York in September 1950 for the commissioning ceremony of the *U.S.S. Oriskany* at the Brooklyn Navy Yard. This was the last of the Essex-class carriers. Only the keel had been laid by the end of World War II, but the Navy decided to finish the ship in anticipation of future needs, giving it some extra armament. While still in port, the ship was attracting a lot of visitors, and there were dances on the hanger deck nearly every night. Hawk got to be one of the "plank owners" – part of the ship's initial crew – and he stayed with the ship for about 18 months at its home port in Quonset Point, Rhode Island and at sea.

The daily schedule started with playing colors (flag-raising to begin the work day), followed by morning rehearsal, early chow (because the band played on the hanger deck while others were in the chow line), dance band rehearsal for two to three hours, an hour off, early chow, and another performance on the hanger deck to play before and between the two evening movies.

That was the routine while sitting in port, and it remain much the same after the ship got underway, except the band didn't play colors in the morning. One of the things Hawk enjoyed the most about his time aboard ship was that he would routinely wake up in the morning in a new country. Flip, the director, would plan rehearsals so that the band worked up material appropriate for the ports they'd be visiting and the events in which they'd be performing.

Like most ships on their shakedown cruise at that time, the *Oriskany* stopped in Guantanamo, Cuba. The crew berthed aboard ship, and the band played marches during the day and a dance at night. Guantanamo had its own band at the base, so the ship's band often joined them to play a midday concert. If the base band played the dance in the evening, the ship's band got the night off.

Marshall was the lead trombonist in a dance band consisting of four trumpets, three trombones, five saxes, and rhythm section. Sometimes the musicians felt that they spent more time and effort setting up, tearing down, and stowing their gear than they did playing music. They didn't have the luxury of leaving that work to "roadies."

The next stop was Brazil, where the *Oriskany* delivered some of the first jets to that country's military. For the band, this began the routine of learning the national anthem for every nation the ship visited. This may sound like a simple task, but it had to be done well to avoid offending foreign officials and guests with a bad rendition. It was also challenging because, as Marshall relates, "some of the anthems are so long it's like learning a symphony. And if we were in port with ships from multiple countries, we had to play the national anthem of all of them when we played colors! That took up a good bit of the morning."

When U.S. Navy ships visited foreign ports, it was quite a spectacle, and the band attracted a lot of attention by playing performances, including dances, for the local population. This often gave the musicians unusual duty hours. Some in the crew didn't understand the band's schedule, and thought the musicians were getting an inordinate amount of free time. On a lot of ships, this caused friction between the bandsmen and the rest of the crew.

The *Oriskany* was headed around the perimeter of South America, eventually arriving on the U.S. west coast where it would change crews before making its way to Korea. The crossing of the equator is a time of ritual for the Navy, or more accurately, a time of misery for new seamen who had never done it before (who were called "pollywogs") and had to endure an initiation. As was the custom, the initiation ceremony was staged by the "shellbacks" who had been across the equator before, and on this trip, a seaman first class was the ringleader. As Marshall recalls, "Part of the punishment – I mean, ritual – involved clubs soaked in sea water that made frequent and violent contact with us pollywogs."

The shellbacks took over the rehearsal area on the hanger deck as their hangout, which was rather inconvenient for the bandsmen. Hawk was the music librarian, so he spent a lot of time there and had work to do. He got annoyed with the shellbacks' frequent demands that he make them coffee. "So I made them a pot of salt water coffee. That earned me the privilege of going through the whole initiation twice."

The initiation ceremony included a royal baby, "the fattest guy on the ship." He greased up his belly with lard and each pollywog had to give it a big kiss. This was followed by a crawl through a pool of sea water and oil. Every time someone tried to get up, one of the tormenters would ask, "What are you, a pollywog or a shellback?" Either answer brought more abuse. Responding "pollywog" got you shoved back into the pool. But claiming to be a shellback brought no relief; the persecutors simply yelled "Not yet!"– and shoved you back into the pool. The grand finale was a "garbage chute" made of parachute silk, complete with garbage. Hawk found that crawling through this mess was enough to make you sick. But when it was over, the shellbacks were kind enough to wash them down – with the full blast of a fire hose. When military recruiters promise unforgettable experiences, they are not kidding.

Having survived the crossing of the equator, the ship traveled around Cape Horn at the southern tip of South America, at which point Hawk became a "Horned" shellback. To his dismay, this was not accompanied by an increase in pay.

Rounding Cape Horn, a destroyer escorted the *Oriskany*. Hawk noticed that sometimes they could only see its mast due to the swells in the rough water. The carrier didn't roll as much as smaller ships, so Hawk didn't get sick during this part of the journey. He was saving that for other occasions. "I was always in better shape above deck, where I could see much of the ship. Below deck, where we were quartered, I felt a close personal relationship with every movement of the ship."

While at sea, the crew could be interrupted at any moment by the sounding of general quarters, at which time they had to report to battle stations. As was the practice during World War II, most bands got assigned to support the medical unit, providing assistance such as stretcher bearer. A couple of bandsmen on this trip did that, but the rest were in damage repair parties. This allowed them to learn a lot about the ship's systems and the procedures for firefighting. Even musicians had to be prepared to go into battle and operate in a degraded environment.

There was still a persistent feeling among many Navy sailors that musicians were elitist and didn't do real work. But the bandsmen wanted to do their part and to change the negative perception. The challenge of improving their image was replayed on each ship and depended on the personalities in the crew and the involvement of leadership.

On some ships, musicians reported to the navigation officer. On cruisers, a typical duty was to stand flight plot watches. The sailor on duty would receive orders coming to the bridge by phone. Standing behind a clear panel, he would write things backwards so those on the other side could read them. Musicians seemed to be better at doing this than others, so they were preferred for that job. It was another educational opportunity on ship operations. But being the go-to guys wasn't always a great learning experience for musicians. In boot camp, for example, they would get stuck teaching the other recruits how to march in step, because they already knew how to do it.

Of course, musicians are best at being musicians, not at handling ammunition or hanging off the side of the ship scraping barnacles. Sometimes another ship would come alongside the carrier, and the band would play while the crew loaded fuel, supplies, or ammunition. But the bandsmen weren't segregated from the rest of the crew. There was plenty of interaction for drills and other activities, including liberty.

The ship stopped for a couple of days in Chile, but there wasn't much activity ashore. As Marshall tells it, "The communists were in control at that time, and there was some unpleasantness going on that we were better off avoiding. We did better in Lima, Peru where we got a good bit of liberty and didn't have much playing to do."

After a stopover in San Francisco, the ship ended up at the Puget Sound Naval Shipyard in

Bremerton, Washington. This was the culmination of Hawk's 18-month assignment aboard the *Oriskany*. Another band was scheduled to accompany the ship to Korea, so the musicians were reassigned and Hawk headed back to the Navy School of Music.

Hawk goes ashore

Marshall was only back at the school for a couple of months. It was decided that he wasn't in need of a refresher course, so he was transferred to the Philadelphia Navy Yard in 1952. This turned out to be an eventful part of his Navy career, and his personal life as well. During his time in Philly he got married, he and his wife had their first child, and he re-enlisted for another six years.

At one time, there had been a dedicated band room at the Navy Yard for the Philadelphia band, but the building had been turned into a dental clinic. The new building assigned to the group only had enough room to store their equipment, so they got permission to use a building across the street for rehearsals. Of course, this resulted in a lot of hauling of equipment back and forth. But the frequent performing opportunities made it worthwhile. Hawk often got to direct concert band and dance band, and to assemble smaller groups for various occasions.

Marshall was the youngest seaman first class in the 23-piece band, which meant he got saddled with a lot of the work. Although it didn't seem like it at the time, this turned out to be a good thing.

Philly was a separation station, so most of the guys who came through there were on their way out. For someone who was still on his way up, this provided a learning experience and an opportunity to make new connections that later paid off.

A series of directors led the band during Marshall's time in Philly. The first was Frank Gardner, who he considered a good director but with an unfortunate inability to control his mouth. For example, one day when the band was playing at a horse show, Frank commented, "This is like a bunch horses' asses coming to watch a bunch of horses' asses." Frank apparently was unaware that he was standing next to an open microphone. He was replaced a short time later by Clark Price. During this time, Marshall experienced an episode that reminded him of ongoing racial tensions in the integrated Navy.

Hawk led a combo (four or five pieces) at a dance in downtown Philly which coincided with the arrival of a submarine in port. The sub's crew was invited to the dance. Hawk was playing bass, and was the only Black member of the group. During the gig, a woman (who happened to be White) asked to sing with the band. She was obviously drunk, and didn't know what she wanted to sing or in what keys she could sing, so Hawk turned her down. A few tunes later, another woman (who happened to be Black) asked to sing. She had specific tunes in mind and knew what keys she wanted, and generally seemed knowledgeable, so she was allowed to sing.

After the band packed up, Hawk was carrying his bass down a hall toward the exit when he was confronted by a big guy from the submarine crew who was clearly plastered. The guy stopped him and said something like, "Why did you let HER sing?!" As one of the very few people on the scene who was sober, perhaps Hawk should have simply backed off and hoped that the intoxicated brute with the unfounded racial grievance would go away. Instead, he put down his bass and walked toward the man, starting to offer an explanation. The immediate response was a punch in the face that knocked Hawk to the ground and made him wonder if he'd need to take inventory of his teeth. Hawk got up and picked up a chair, and at the same time, the band's drummer, a burly guy who had been a timber cutter, came to his aid. There was no shore patrol around, but suddenly three men who were probably his shipmates grabbed the big guy and pulled him away. Hawk could see from his stripes that he was a seaman with about 12 years of experience, and he wanted to get his name and serial number so he could report the incident. However, nobody was willing to provide the information, and the room cleared out in a flash. Eventually, a lieutenant commander intervened to do damage control, but Hawk still didn't learn the identity of his attacker.

The following Monday morning, band director Clark Price took one look at Marshall with his bruised face and out-of-kilter nose and he went ballistic. Price was a trumpet player and a tough guy, not well liked by most people. But Marshall got along with him, and Price took care of him that day. They went straight to the admiral's office, which contacted the submarine, still in port. That led to a lineup of the crew in which Marshall easily picked out the guy who slugged him. Marshall surmised that this probably wasn't the first time the guy had been in this kind of trouble. He was still a seaman after about 12 years of service, and he had a history of alcohol abuse and hostility issues. Later that day, he tried to apologize to Hawk by phone, and then in person. But Marshall didn't drop the complaint because "I have little tolerance for people who get hammered and then lose control and become aggressive." Hawk didn't hear what eventually happened to him, other than that he faced a court martial hearing.

There were other examples of the sad state of race relations during Marshall's time in Philly. He had a couple more directors before leaving that assignment, and last one was a seaman first class named Stone, a slightly built Black man who smoked a corncob pipe. He didn't care much for White people and frequently referred to them as "palefaces." Soon after Marshall moved on to his next assignment, Stone retired and went to live in Japan. Marshall speculated that "Maybe he had a greater affinity for Japanese culture than for White America."

One of the lessons learned in Philadelphia was that things don't always go as planned. For example, the Navy Yard musicians played a variety of jobs across a wide area, using either a big band or a five- or six-piece combo. One day they went to Wilmington, Delaware to play on a radio show with a small group. Hawk was in charge, and was going to play trombone. When the group got to the location and started unloading, he discovered that his trombone was missing. Someone else was supposed to load it, and they had neglected to do so. Hawk did what jazz musicians do: improvise. He would play piano instead. The problem was that although he could plunk out chords, he wasn't an accomplished piano player, "so I did as much talking as possible to minimize my playing."

Back to sea

When the assignment was done in Philadelphia, it was back to shipboard duty. Hawk headed down to Norfolk, Virginia to join the *U.S.S. Pocono*, a communications ship. The first cruise was to Jamaica, and for the first time, he got seasick. The ship bounced around in rough seas a lot more than the carrier had done.

The *Pocono* participated in a lot of exercises for things like amphibious landings, and the bandsmen found themselves in a different type of assignment. Rather than being stretcher bearers or repairmen, they helped handle the communications, relaying messages and learning a lot about another aspect of naval operations.

The ship's band director was Donald "Ducky" DeMoss. Hawk found him to be an exceptionally nice guy, but he seemed to be "scared of his shadow and didn't seem to have much backbone." Hawk later learned something that may have contributed to that trepidation: Ducky had been in the Bataan death march in the Philippines during World War II. DeMoss soon was replaced by Nathan "Flip" Flippin, who had been Hawk's band director on the *Oriskany*.

The *Pocono* went to the Mediterranean to become part of the 6th fleet. During travels there, the bandsmen often interacted with musicians from other ships, included many Navy School of Music alumni. The band's baritone sax player also was able to interact with his wife, who came to Europe and made her way from port to port, following the ship. Young love on full display! Later, she published a book based on their love letters during his Navy years.

To make some extra money, some of the bandsmen sold cigarettes. They would purchase them cheaply aboard ship, and then take them ashore by loading cartons of them inside the bass drum. They'd sell the cigarettes on the local black market, and then fill the empty bass drum with bottles of booze to take back to the ship. Nobody checked the band's gear when they came back on board, so they got away with it, although it must have looked funny when two guys were struggling to carry an unusually heavy bass drum.

Teaching and directing the Navy's finest musicians

In 1956, Marshall returned from the Mediterranean on the *Pocono* and went back to the Navy School of Music to take the advanced course. After eight or nine months, he had the opportunity to take the test for promotion to chief petty officer, which the music program called chief musician. He passed the test and got the promotion in September 1957. Of course, Marshall was happy to move up in rank and get a pay raise, but he was surprised to find that many people assigned special significance to his promotion. He felt they were "going overboard" because he was the first Black man to achieve the rank of chief musician. He didn't see this as such a big deal because racial competition had never been emphasized in his family or elsewhere in his experience. He just took it in stride, and never dwelled on its importance – except for that pay raise, of course.

Marshall understood how some people felt. A retired colleague – another African-American who had been drafted into the Navy before it was integrated and remembered what it was like – was thrilled when he heard about the promotion. It meant so much to him that he invited Marshall to visit the school band he was directing. Marshall found himself in a room full of kids looking at him as a role model. He found it very touching that they had made him an award certificate.

Becoming chief came with its own initiation ceremony, although it was somewhat less disgusting than the ordeal of crossing the equator as a pollywog. Despite finding the practice repulsive, Hawk was not above playing a role in the hazing when it was his turn to be among the antagonists. Later on, a fellow teacher named Dick Raven became chief. Unlike most of the guys, he did not consume alcohol. During his initiation, as Hawk described it, "he was required to eat some horrible slop, so I poured a big glass of vodka, set it down in front of him, and said, 'Here, Dick, you're going to need a glass of water to wash that down.' I don't think he ever forgave me for that one."

From this description of Marshall's rise to chief musician, it may seem that successful completion of the school's advanced class would quickly earn a promotion and a new and better assignment. But typically it was a much longer process. Usually, there was yet another shipboard assignment, then a period of waiting until the next opportunity to take the exam for chief musician along with everyone else who was eligible. That could result in a long delay between graduation and a promotion to be leader of an ensemble. Marshall saw this as an unnecessary disincentive to aspiring bandleaders.

Marshall witnessed an example of how sluggish a career track can be. Al Beck and Phil Field were students in his advanced class in the late 1960s. Al became the director of the U.S. Navy Band in 1984-89 – almost two decades later. He was followed in that position by Phil in 1989-92. Eighteen years after his retirement, Marshall attended the change-of-command ceremony between the two. At one point, he asked both of them to speak with him privately in the office so he could tell them how proud he was of their accomplishments. Al evidently was expecting something different, because he burst into the room and said, "Okay, Hawk, what did I do wrong this time?" That cracked everybody up – as did Hawk's realization that the room he'd known as the office was now the men's lavatory.

As an instructor at the School of Music, Hawk was considered a taskmaster, something he was proud of even though it temporarily earned him the nickname Crusader Rabbit. He felt that he really needed to push his students because the Navy was making a big investment in their training and equipment, and then sending them all over the world to represent the United States.

Expectations were high. The advanced class attempted to cram the equivalent of three years of a college music major into one year. There was little time for anything else. In addition to classes, rehearsals, and personal practicing – usually on more than one instrument – students had to attend concerts of other military bands and related events, take notes on them, and write them up. This training schedule may not sound especially challenging, but about a third of the people who passed the audition for the advanced class washed out before the first quarter was over. Around two-thirds would be gone by the end of the year. But the ones that were left really knew their stuff. Some of the other instructors were uneasy about the number of students who burned out in Hawk's classes, but his response was, "Well, if you don't like the way I'm doing this, I can transfer to another assignment. I'm ready to go tomorrow!" Nobody ever suggested that he transfer.

One of the points that Marshall would hammer into his students almost daily was that they should have the courage to go up against captains, even though they could always be overruled. As he reminded them, the band directors were the ones responsible for the Navy's investment in its musicians and their equipment. Directors who wouldn't assert themselves would have a hard time winning the respect of their musicians. That was a consistent message throughout the 14 advanced classes that Marshall supervised.

During his time on the faculty, Hawk did a lot of writing for the ensembles. At that time, arrangers were not permitted to take their equipment and supplies and work at home. He was stuck in a tiny, stuffy, windowless room at the base. Often he had to come up with arrangements quickly, sometimes in just a couple of days. That involved some late nights listening to songs, playing with fresh ideas, and scribbling out a score. Copyists were available to write out the individual parts from the score, but sometimes they had only one day to do so. The demanding schedule made him feel like he was writing music for weekly television shows.

Hawk sometimes got assigned to lead ensembles for special military or public events. Some of them seem anachronistic today. For example, one Saturday, he led a group that played for a soap box derby competition on Pennsylvania Avenue in downtown DC, between Alabama Avenue and Minnesota Avenue. Today, most people don't even remember what the soap box derby was, and can't imaging closing down DC streets for such an event, even on a Saturday.

One day in 1960, Hawk was tasked with taking one of the four bands he was directing to play at an event in a northern Virginia suburb of DC. The band had about 40 players. In addition to Hawk, three of them were African-Americans and the rest were White.

It was early in the day, and as usual the band had to show up before the performance to set up. They were ready with time to spare, and there hadn't been time for breakfast, so Marshall let everybody go to a nearby drugstore to get something to eat. (In those days, drugstores still had lunch counters.) He noticed that the three Black musicians weren't going with the rest of the group. He asked them, "Aren't you guys going to get something to eat?" They replied, "No thanks, Chief, we're fine."

Hawk headed over to the drugstore, arriving behind the rest of his group. Some of them were already getting served. When he sat down with them, one of the servers said, "I'm sorry, we can't serve you here – you'll have to go around to the window in the back." It took Hawk a second to realize that he was being given the Jim Crow treatment. Meanwhile, this comment had been overheard by the band's drummer, a seaman first class from California, who quietly got up and walked past the other guys, whispering to them. Then something happened that Hawk never expected: they all got up and calmly walked out, leaving their food on the table. It was a great expression of solidarity among the bandsmen, and of the respect they showed for their chief.

Hawk had been so wrapped up in his music and his military duties that he had largely tuned out the racial tensions in the rest of society. The drugstore incident caught him off guard, and his reaction was, "I don't know what surprised me more: the denial of service at the lunch counter, or the immediate and unanimous rejection of racial prejudice by the White musicians under my command."

Tightening up on testing

Prior to about 1950, testing of musicians in the Navy had been pretty loose. Marshall heard stories that provide some examples. In one case, a supervisor told a musician that he was needed to lead a band, and he replied that he couldn't because he hadn't taken the chief musician exam yet. The ensuing conversation went something like this:

"What instrument do you play?"
"Trumpet."

"How many valves does a trumpet have?"
"Three."
"Correct. Okay, you're a chief."

In another story, a tuba player was asked to play the lower brass interlude from the Stars and Stripes Forever march, which he did competently. That was reportedly followed by:

"Do you play string bass?"
"Yes."
"Play a walking bass line for a blues progression." Again, competently performed.
"Okay, sew another stripe on your uniform."

Things became much more stringent by the time Marshall came along. The exams required of the musicians were meticulously planned out and were very challenging.

After he had been teaching the advanced course in DC for a few years, Marshall was offered the job of directing the Navy music exam center in Great Lakes. That would mean moving the family again, but it seemed like the right job at the right time, so he headed for Illinois. Upon arrival, he found that the only piece of equipment that the exam writers had was a first-generation electric piano. He raised a fuss about all the other things that were needed, such as reference books, recordings, and a record player. Eventually, he put together a usable set-up.

Marshall found that some of his colleagues at the exam center were not using the most up-to-date terminology on the exams. They were conforming to traditional musical vocabulary rather than using terms that appeared routinely in the real world. Also, he was surprised to find that when exams were given at various locations away from Great Lakes, no one from the exam center bothered to attend. There was no supervision of how the tests were administered, even though they had audio as well as written components. There was no formal or informal collection of feedback from the test-takers. He believed that had to change, so twice a year at exam time he'd travel to the sites where they were being administered to see what he could learn.

On one occasion, Marshall wasn't feeling well after he returned from a trip to an exam site. He attributed this to his tendency, like many other servicemen, to do a little bit of extra drinking while on temporary duty away from home base. Soon, however, he was "spewing out some really vile stuff from both ends." He went to his commander and calmly announced, "I think I'm bleeding internally." At the base hospital, he was diagnosed with a bleeding ulcer and stayed there for the next 31 days. The hospital poked, prodded, plugged him into intravenous drips, and kept him on steady consumption of "some kind of unpalatable milky liquid." Marshall was convinced that the ulcer healed itself, and the hospital's only function was to prevent him from behaving (or consuming) in ways that would make things worse.

Directing ensembles again

After recovering from that health scare – and after working at the exam center from 1963 to 1967 – it was time for another change. The Navy had formed a band in London that was transferred to Naples, Italy to become the NATO band. Marshall was sent to Naples to be its director and stayed there from 1967 to 1969.

Hawk returned to the DC area to lead the newly formed Commodores, the Navy's premier jazz ensemble. One of the first engagements the Commodores performed was at the White House in April 1969 when President Richard Nixon awarded the Presidential Medal of Freedom to Duke Ellington. The Duke was the first jazz musician and the first African-American to receive this high honor. (Other jazz musicians receiving the same honor include Eubie Blake in 1981, Count Basie in 1985, Ella Fitzgerald in 1992, Arturo Sandoval in 2013.)

Celebrity encounters

Duke Ellington wasn't the only jazz celebrity that Hawk encountered during his Navy career. At one point, he did some gigs with the well-known jazz drummer Cozy Cole. A talented guy who also did some singing, Cozy was quite a character. He was fond of standing up at some point during the evening, spreading his arms wide and bellowing, "Is everybody happy!" For most gigs, this would prompt a joyous response from the audience, which was half-crocked by this time. But once, while playing for a bar mitzvah, Cozy's exuberant shout brought dead silence from the crowd. They probably didn't know what to make of him. The rest of the band told him that maybe he'd better cool it for the rest of the evening.

One of the most memorable encounters took place in the early 1950s, near the *Oriskany*'s home port in Rhode Island. Hawk and three of his Navy band buddies (two trumpeters and a drummer) often would hang out together, checking out jazz clubs in the region. Sometimes they'd get to sit in with the club's band for a couple of tunes, for which Hawk would typically play string bass.

One night they made their way to the Celebrity Club in Providence, where the featured act was a duo consisting of legendary pianist Art Tatum and bassist Slam Stewart. Hawk had seen Tatum perform in DC a number of times, and after a round of drinks, he and the guys worked up the courage to introduce themselves and ask if they could sit in. Tatum welcomed them to the stage, so they were getting their wish to jam with a master. By this time, Slam Stewart was drunk, slumped over the bar. He was done for the evening. This made his bass available for Hawk to play. Not that Art Tatum really needed a bass player.

They briefly discussed what tunes to play, and decided to start with St. Louis Blues. This made Jesse, one of the trumpeters, very happy because he had been featured on that tune in an arrangement in the Navy band's dance book. He figured he'd have a smooth ride and be able to play an impressive solo.

The arrangement Jesse was familiar with in the dance book was a slow, lazy blues. But Tatum kicked off the tune at breakneck speed, and everyone had to do their best to keep up. Jesse backed away, grabbed his bottle of valve oil, and slowly began unscrewing the valves on his trumpet and meticulously oiling them. He did that for the whole tune and never played a note. George, the other trumpeter, leaped into the breach and got himself a good piece of the solo space.

A musician's work is never done

Marshall's 22-year Navy career ended in 1971, but the former Master Chief Musician continued life as a civilian musician and bandleader. His experience and enthusiasm kept him going well into his 80s, until he was confronted by the restrictions of the coronavirus pandemic. For decades, he remained active with Navy band alumni activities and ran his own piano tuning service. By his own admission, Marshall was never a skilled pianist, but he was an active member of the Piano Technicians Guild, a professional association that certifies piano repair and tuning specialists. Applying his Navy exam center experience, he was a key player in the development of the Guild's testing regimen.

Marshall was a prominent and respected leader in the U.S. military's most influential music organization: the Navy School of Music, which has trained Army and Marine musicians as well as the Navy's own. He continued to inspire musicians in civilian life, including me and many others that I've observed. He was already 80 by the time I met him, yet in the years that followed I frequently heard colleagues say, after he had led a rehearsal, "I like it when Marshall directs. He always gets the best out of us."

References

Bayes, Michael P. "Pioneers of Navy music: A history of African-Americans in the Navy Music Program," *Fanfare Online*, March/April 2011, Volume 32 Number 2, United States Navy Band (http://www.navyband.navy.mil/fanfare_online_mar_apr_2011.shtml).

Jones, Patrick M. *A History of the Armed Forces School of Music*, Pennsylvania State University Press, 2002, 483 pages.

Jones, Patrick M. "The Naval School of Music: Relevant Training for Real-World Musical Missions," *Music Educators Journal*, March 2015, pp. 47-54 (http://veterans.syr.edu/wp-content/uploads/2015/03/Jones-Naval-School-of-Music-MEJ-March-2015.pdf).

Kent, Molly. *USS Arizona's last band: The history of U.S. Navy Band Number 22*, Silent Song Books, 1996 (http://www.amazon.com/USS-Arizonas-last-band-history/dp/0965419908/ref=pd_rhf_dp_p_img_2?ie=UTF8&refRID=1VKAK7Y320APSKZR7T4Z).

U.S. Naval Institute, "Navy Bands: Diversity in Action" (https://www.navalhistory.org/2019/11/12/navy-bands-diversity-in-action).

Peters, Rosemary. "After Arizona: Military Musicians in the Second World War," LISA e-journal, Vol. X, No. 1, 2012, pp. 209-234 (https://lisa.revues.org/4994).

Chapter 2

The Ubiquitous Marvin Stamm

When I was coming of age as an aspiring jazz player in the 1970s, building a record collection was a key element of my education. Listening to a variety of artists and styles was important, but so was reading the liner notes on the albums — a learning experience that sadly is missing for those who rely entirely on digital downloads. Well-written liner notes provided a wealth of information on the artists, the arrangers, the recording sessions, the selection of tunes, and relevant jazz history.

At the listening sessions I frequented with my brother and our musically-inclined friends, we compared the personnel listed in the liner notes of our piles of albums, and a pattern emerged. It seemed that every album with trumpets on it that was recorded in New York included the name Marvin Stamm. His name appeared so frequently that we wondered how one person could be on so many sessions in such a short period of time. We jokingly speculated that Marvin Stamm wasn't actually a real person, but rather a made-up name that album cover designers inserted in the list of personnel when they couldn't remember the names of all the trumpeters.

Today, I can verify that Marvin Stamm is a real person. But I didn't get to see him perform live until 2006 in a concert that I almost missed, even though it took place less than three miles from my home.

My wife and I saw the sign outside nearby Thomas Edison High School in Alexandria, Virginia. All it said was that an orchestra from the University of Tennessee would be performing in the school's auditorium on February 14, which gave us something fun to do on Valentine's Day. To our surprise, the concert featured two prominent guest artists: Marvin Stamm and pianist Bill Mays. We had seen no other advertising aside from the sign in front of the school, which should have displayed their names in flashing red lights. It was a great show in every way – the soloists, the orchestra, the music selection. The concert was memorable for those reasons, but also because it began my acquaintance with Marvin and reinvigorated my interest in his extensive career accomplishments.

From the home of the blues to a Texas training ground

Marvin started playing trumpet in junior high school at age 12. He had excellent training through high school, but there was no jazz ensemble. He became interested in jazz through the record collection of his older brother, who was not a musician but nonetheless became his first jazz influence. Playing along with the records developed his "ear" and stimulated his interest in improvisation. This activity, along with training in concert bands, carried him through his teen years.

This enthusiastic youngster from Memphis entered a whole new world when he began his studies at North Texas State University (now the University of North Texas, UNT). He pursued his trumpet performance degree from 1957 to 1961, playing in the lab band, concert band, and orchestra. He found himself among students from around the country, most of them older and more experienced, including some veterans of the Korean War.

Marvin was interested in all the ensembles available to him at the school, but particularly the jazz lab band program. Gene Hall, creator of the first university degree program in jazz, was the director of the program for Marvin's first two years. During Dr. Hall's tenure, the band participated in concerts and festivals mostly in Texas, and occasionally in other nearby areas.

When Dr. Hall left for another university, he recommended Leon Breeden to take over his position leading the jazz program. When Breeden took over the program, he enlarged the band's reach and recognition. He initially sought to expand beyond Texas to nearby states such as Oklahoma, Arkansas, and Missouri. As a result of these efforts, the jazz band received an invitation in spring 1960 to compete in a jazz festival hosted by Notre Dame University. This turned out to be a turning point for North Texas, and for Marvin in particular, because the band was declared the best ensemble at the festival and Marvin was awarded best trumpeter and best instrumentalist.

One of the festival's judges was bandleader Stan Kenton, and the prize for the winners was attendance at a Kenton jazz clinic to be held that summer at Indiana University. Marvin had already made a commitment to go on the road with trombonist Buddy Morrow's band that summer, but left the tour in time to attend the August clinic. (Years later, Marvin often worked with Morrow in the New York studio scene.)

In those early incarnations of the week-long Kenton clinics, Stan did not bring his band. So for part of August 1960, the North Texas crew became his band. They played arrangements from his library at concerts, led by one of the most widely recognized and respected big band leaders of the time. After hearing Marvin play for him all week, Kenton asked him to join his band for its next tour.

Have trumpet, will travel

Kenton's offer posed a dilemma because Marvin had one more academic year left until graduation. He couldn't envision coming this far in his studies without finishing his bachelor's degree. And his parents – neither of whom went beyond high school – were counting on him to get his degree. He politely declined the offer, and Stan was very understanding. But he wasn't quite done with the talented young trumpeter.

Just two months later, Stan was in need of a replacement for trumpeter Sam Noto, who had decided to end his road gigs and settle in New York City. Stan called on Marvin to finish the tour, if he could get a leave of absence from his classes for three or four weeks. Marvin consulted with his professors, who all told him to go for it. He was able to hit the road, with maybe a little bit of studying to do along the way.

When the tour ended, the Kenton band was scheduled for a four-month break. Stan's next question was, "When do you graduate?" The answer was early May 1961, a few weeks after the band's next tour would begin. Stan arranged to have a temporary player for those first weeks, after which Marvin would have his seat in the Kenton trumpet section. Over the next two years, he would play on five Kenton albums.

This edition of the Kenton band was known as the Mellophonium Orchestra because the standard big band instrumentation was supplemented by four mellophoniums – redesigned mellophones with their bells facing front like a trumpet rather than off to the side like a French horn. They were quirky horns that were difficult to play in tune, and they brought a new challenge to the band's arrangers, who had to write for an additional horn section. The charts tended to be heavy and loud, and some felt they didn't swing. "Balls-to-the-wall most of the time, which Stan loved," as Marvin recalls. The band had a unique concert-jazz sound that appealed to many in its fan base. Although some listeners found it to be too intense, the brief tenure of Kenton's Mellophonium Orchestra still holds a special place in the hearts of many big band aficionados.

Although this was a productive time, there were obstacles. After the 1961 tour, Marvin was experiencing some discomfort with his embouchure. He consulted John Haynie, his former North Texas trumpet professor, regarding the problem. Haynie felt the solution was to play with the mouthpiece a bit higher on the lips. As any brass player who has gone through this can testify, it can take weeks or months to fully adjust to such a change; Marvin believes it took him two years to complete the transition. When the 1962 touring schedule got underway, there were some rough moments. Stan was sympathetic, and told Marvin, "I know you're having a tough time. Don't worry about it. Just focus on what you do when you go up to the mic for the solos. Don't worry about the section parts."

Marvin found Stan to be a generous and understanding gentleman, and a pleasure to work with. But their relationship would be tested after the band's second 1962 tour.

Marvin got married right out of college, and immediately hit the road with Kenton. Musicians have a long history of struggling with the inherent incompatibility between marriages and road gigs, and that was clearly evident in Marvin's case. After the eight-month tour in 1962, he wrote to Stan explaining that his marriage was over, and he would need to step away from the band until he could get his personal life in order. He left the band at the beginning of 1963, and had the impression that Stan was unhappy about this, much as a mentor would be disappointed in a student who suddenly broke off a relationship, or a father would be frustrated with an errant son. This type of reaction was not unusual for bandleaders who relied on and had become attached to their sidemen.

In addition to the personal issues, the road work proved financially unfulfilling as well. At the end of 1962, after months of touring at a salary of about $200 a week, Marvin had about $300 in the bank. Also, he was facing the possibility that there would be little or no work for several months. It was imperative to go out and hunt for work, so he headed to New York City.

New connections, new opportunities

In the early 1960s, it was much cheaper to travel. In the big cities, you could find a decent hotel room for a few dollars a night, and could reduce expenses by sharing with fellow musicians. But wages were low, so money was still tight.

Within a couple of days of arriving in the Big Apple, Marvin got a call to play with Lionel Hampton's band, which was going to Washington, DC to play for a large industrial show at one of the area's convention centers. (These types of shows continue today, but rarely feature live music.) Three days into the gig, he woke up experiencing blurred vision and realized he was unable to play. His friends in the band put him on an airplane to Memphis so he could recuperate at the home of his parents. When he got there, it was determined that he had a case of walking pneumonia as well as an impacted wisdom tooth.

After he recovered, Marvin got a call in February 1963 from drummer Dave Barry, a close friend from his North Texas days, offering a steady gig in Houston. Dave was playing with a hotel house band that frequently served as the backup band for big-name performers who came to town, such as singers Robert Goulet and Edie Adams. The band's 2nd trumpeter had to leave due to illness, so a spot was open for Marvin if he wanted it – and he took it.

Two weeks after arriving in Houston, Marvin's wife, now separated from him, contacted him and announced that she was no longer able to take care of their daughter, who was not yet two years old. Marvin took custody, and was fortunate to have the help of Dave and his wife, who had a daughter about the same age. Together, they made arrangements to share household duties and expenses and take care of the kids. The two musical fathers performed in the evenings and played Mr. Mom during the day.

The Houston gig only lasted until early May, when the band's ailing trumpeter recovered and came back to work. Marvin, with his daughter, headed back to Memphis, where he tapped into his local contacts to get recording work, mostly for "jingles" (radio commercials and call-signs), and to do some shows. Sadly, in August, he had to give up his daughter when his wife demanded that custody be returned to her.

Marvin worked as an instructor at the summer Kenton clinics for several years. This helped him keep in touch with his old Kenton band colleagues. One of them, saxophonist Charlie Mariano, asked Marvin to come to New York in fall 1963 to help him record an album. This turned out to be more elaborate than a standard jazz quintet effort. The album, *Portrait of an Artist*, had three settings: quintet; Charlie with a string quartet and rhythm section; and Charlie with a brass section. The arranger for the album was trombonist Don Sebesky, whose writing is well known even today among players with experience in large jazz ensembles. As the "guy from out of town" sitting in with a group of New York regulars, Marvin was surprised and gratified at how welcoming they were, and how enjoyable the whole experience was. It was here that he met trumpeter Bernie Glow, a seasoned studio player who would become a friend and mentor a few years later when Marvin returned to New York.

From there it was back to Memphis and the radio jingles. Before long, Marvin again heard from Dave Barry, who was now working in Reno, Nevada. Although less famous than Las Vegas, Reno in early 1964 was a city of hotels and casinos which provided a lot of work for musicians playing shows. As before, he and Dave's family were able to make some mutually supportive living arrangements, this time including sharing a house.

As in Las Vegas and some other large cities, Reno's musicians union had a six-month residency requirement before players could take a steady engagement. They could take individual gigs ("one-nighters") but could not sign on to an ongoing contract until they had their full union membership. Marvin was able to play in "relief" bands that performed when house bands had the night off. This turned out to be great sight-reading practice because relief players didn't have much rehearsal time and had to master their parts quickly.

Marvin enjoyed his time in Reno. He made a lot of friends among the great players there and felt enriched by his many challenging musical experiences. Reno was part of a show circuit (along with Las Vegas and Lake Tahoe) that attracted many notable performers that Marvin backed up, including Louis Armstrong, Dean Martin, Sammy Davis Jr., Nancy Wilson, and Pearl Bailey (whose husband was the great jazz drummer Louie Bellson).

Don't get too comfortable

While in Reno, Marvin befriended a saxophonist named Dave Matthews. Dave was an older musician who had worked with Harry James and other bands early on, but was now working in Reno show bands. One evening, over drinks after work, Matthews challenged Marvin by asking, "What are you doing here?" The question was unclear at first, but Dave followed up with "What are you doing in Reno? Do you want to do this the rest of your life? If you do, this could be your graveyard. You should get the fuck out of here." Marvin acknowledged that he eventually intended to move on, but Matthews wasn't satisfied. He replied, "Oh yeah? I'll tell you what – a year from today, if I see you walking down the street, I'm going to bust you in the nose." Since this was coming from a good friend (although one who was a bit inebriated), Marvin took it as incentive to be more ambitious, and appreciated the demonstration of tough-love mentoring from someone who cared.

In September 1965, Marvin got a call from trumpeter Bill Chase inviting him to join Woody Herman's band, where he stayed for nearly a year (fall 1965 to summer 1966). Woody's personality and style were different from Stan Kenton. He was less fatherly than Stan, but Marvin found him to be a great musician and a great bandleader.

In the months Marvin played with Woody's band, nearly half of the time was spent touring overseas. They performed in France, Spain, Germany, and also took part in the U.S. State Department's Jazz Ambassadors program (a Cold War cultural outreach effort that ran from the mid-1950s to the late 1970s). For 10 weeks in 1966, they toured Africa and Eastern Europe, including performances in Morocco, Tunisia, Egypt, the Ivory Coast, Tanzania, Uganda, and the Congo (just weeks before an attempted coup in that country). These appearances were followed by stops in Bucharest, Romania and Belgrade, Yugoslavia.

Marvin thoroughly enjoyed his time with the Herman band – the people, the music, and the experiences both on and off the stage. The band was hot, and was really swinging. But it was hard work. There could be hundreds of miles between engagements, and the schedule was tight. Marvin opined that "When you're on the road with Woody, you're really on the road... It's a good thing I was single at that time."

Back to the Big Apple

By mid-1966, Marvin was 27 years old and felt it was time to set a new course for his career. He decided to move to New York City for a variety of reasons. He remembered the positive experience he had there while recording Charlie Mariano's album. Also, he was attracted to the many players and arrangers who lived and worked there, such as Gil Evans, Bob Brookmeyer, Manny Albam, Snooky Young, Thad Jones, Frank Foster, Frank Wess, and Ernie Royal. Los Angeles also had many great players, and he had spent time there during his stint with Kenton, but for him it didn't have the same appeal.

Marvin prepared to move to New York in November 1966 with $3,500 in his pocket, which he figured would sustain him for six months or more while he tried to find his place in the city's music scene. His commitment to this new path was tested in the weeks prior to departure when he was contacted by both the Harry James and Count Basie bands with offers to join them for tours. Both offers were very tempting, but he decided to stick to the plan.

Upon arriving in New York, Marvin checked into a hotel that he was familiar with from his travels with the Kenton and Herman bands. Nearby there was a watering hole called Jim & Andy's where many of the jazz and studio players hung out. When touring, Marvin hadn't worked up the nerve to hang with that crowd, but as a new arrival on the scene it was important to meet other musicians there.

On his first day in town, he walked into Jim & Andy's and found it quiet – no one there other than the bartender and one person sitting at the bar. He seemed to have chosen the wrong time for networking opportunities with fellow musicians.

Despite this, he went up to the bar and ordered a cup of coffee. The gentleman sitting a couple of stools away asked him if he was new in town, and Marvin told him, "Yes, I just flew in today." The next question would have seemed odd in most places, but not in a jazz hangout in NYC: "Are you a musician?" Marvin acknowledged that he was a trumpeter, whereupon the friendly stranger shook his hand and said, "I am too. My name is Ernie Royal." By pure luck, Marvin's first networking effort had put him face-to-face with one of his heroes.

Ernie Royal was one of the top lead trumpet players in NYC, having appeared on dozens of albums with many noted artists. At the time, he was a staff musician with the ABC television network and one of the busiest freelancers in town. (Later, he would play in the *Tonight Show* band on the NBC network.) If Marvin had decided to turn around and leave when he saw the nearly empty bar, he would have missed a chance encounter with a fellow trumpeter who would become a close friend and mentor.

That afternoon, Ernie taught Marvin a lot about the freelance music scene. He suggested an answering service for musicians that Marvin immediately joined, and he got a call from the service a week later. Jimmy Nottingham, another prolific trumpeter who was a staff musician with the CBS network, had come down with the flu. Marvin was asked to substitute for him in the Thad Jones-Mel Lewis band at their regular

Monday night gig at the Village Vanguard. That was the beginning of a six-and-a-half year relationship with Thad & Mel. After that first gig, they asked Marvin to be the "swing" player for the trumpet section – in other words, he became the on-call substitute who would play any one of the four books as needed. After about a year, he became a regular member of the trumpet section.

Thad & Mel's band didn't travel much because the band was made up of busy studio players. But they did go on a brief European tour in 1969. The tour also included a quartet that featured Freddie Hubbard on trumpet.

One night after a concert in Stuttgart, Germany, the band was invited to a jam session at a local pub. After the playing had started, Freddie showed up with a young lady on each arm. It was evident that he already had been partying and was feeling it. He sat down right in front of the stage. When the tune finished, he walked over to Marvin and said, "Gimme your horn!" Marvin handed him his horn and sat on sidelines as Freddie played. After he finished, Freddie apparently was aware that he had not delivered his best performance. He got off the stage and angrily thrust the horn back at Marvin.

The next morning, as the musicians boarded a plane for their next stop, Freddie came up behind Marvin and said menacingly, "You got me last night, but that won't happen again." Marvin didn't take his threatening manner seriously, and he later played in the trumpet section on a couple of Freddie's albums for the CTI label.

Working with Thad & Mel was a great experience, both for playing and for linking up with more musicians. Connections were important because most work in New York came through "word of mouth" advertising – musicians telling others about new players in town. At first, a lot of the calls were for rehearsal bands, but this quickly led to performance gigs and recording sessions, and it wasn't long before Marvin became a regular in the studios.

Although he was keeping busy, Marvin took time off each summer to visit his daughter in California. On those trips, he developed a friendship with Mannie Klein, a first-call trumpeter for Los Angeles recording studios whose resumé of jazz, classical, and movie soundtrack recording extended back to the big band era. Marvin was staying at Mannie's home when he met Nancy, whom he would marry in 1972 after a long-distance relationship. Five decades later, they are still together.

Live from the studios

Another chance meeting illustrates the importance of whom you know – and of just plain luck. About six months after settling in New York, Marvin was walking down the street one day and happened to meet Bernie Glow. Although they had only seen each other at the Charlie Mariano recording date four years earlier, Bernie recognized him and said, "Marvin, what are you doing here?" When Marvin told him that he was now living in New York, Bernie said, "Why haven't you called me?" Imagine being asked that question by one of your longtime heroes – that's how Marvin felt at that moment. It was the beginning of a close friendship that lasted until Bernie's passing in 1982. The two trumpeters played many recording sessions together as the older, more established musician helped to open doors for the young newcomer.

Bernie was one of the many colleagues who helped Marvin's career by recommending him for gigs. He was a modest man despite his prominence on the studio scene. On a session one day, Marvin mentioned to Bernie that so many players had helped him get established in New York. Marvin asked, "How does one repay such generosity?" Bernie's response was, "When a new player comes to town, you do the same thing for the next generation of talented musicians." Pass it along. That was one of the guiding principles that Marvin adopted for his own career evolution and for the long-term prosperity of his profession.

Once accepted as a member of the music community, a player's reputation can spread quickly. In his first year, Marvin had over 225 recording sessions – an impressive amount of work for someone new on the scene.

Building a good reputation hinges on some key characteristics. The first, of course, is good playing and sight-reading abilities that can "deliver the goods" in a variety of musical settings. Equally important is what Marvin calls the "behavior" aspect. A musician has to be reliable, showing up on time and in good condition to play, and has to have a personality that promotes smooth interaction with other session participants.

A behavioral standard emphasized by Ernie Royal and Bernie Glow was the importance of showing respect to other players. Frequently, new players who were eager to make an impression failed to respect those around them. They would swagger into a session insistent on getting the solos or the lead chair, setting a bad tone from the start. Marvin found that if you show deference to others, especially those who are more experienced, they will make sure that you have interesting parts to play, eventually leading to your turn in the spotlight.

From Marvin's description of the atmosphere among New York studio musicians, it was a fellowship of competent professionals characterized by mutual respect and enduring social relationships. He vividly remembers stories that illustrate the talents and personalities of many of his colleagues from that time. For example, he recalls that Marky Markowitz, despite his extensive experience, always sat in the lowest chair of the trumpet section. If one of the other trumpeters was getting tired on a long session, they could ask Marky to cover their part, confident that he'd do it beautifully.

Marvin and Marky once played on a session that was recording music for a short film for a corporate customer. The composer had to make the music accentuate certain "hits" in the video but he didn't use a click track for synchronization. Later, the film's editors changed the timing on the video, making all the music hits happen in the wrong places. The composer adjusted his music to compensate and then called out a series of corrections to the players such as "add a beat to bar five... change bar twelve to a 2/4 bar... extend bar thirty-two to cover two bars..." and so on. Everyone frantically penciled in the changes – except Marky. He just sat there looking at his music, and when it came time to record, he played all the changes perfectly from memory.

When Marvin moved to New York, there was a good racial mix among studio musicians. At least half of the players were white, but there were many Black and Latino players, and everyone worked well together. Typically, no one knew who would be on a session with them until they arrived at the studio. The arrangers often requested specific musicians for their sessions, but race was rarely a relevant factor.

Marvin remembers hearing from guys on the road who wished they could cut back on touring, increase their income, and achieve more stability. Typically, while on tour, they got a small weekly paycheck and nothing else – no medical benefits, no contributions to the musicians union pension fund, nothing sufficient to support a family and build a future. Studio work could solve this, but road musicians faced significant barriers to entry. Being on the road made them unavailable for studio calls, which often came on short notice, and prevented them from taking the necessary steps to build their reputation.

In the 1960s and 70s, there were a lot of sessions for big band or full orchestra with arrangements written by Ralph Burns, Manny Albam, J.J. Johnson, Patrick Williams, Oliver Nelson, and many other great writers. Marvin often had three studio gigs in a single day, and with the shorter jingle sessions, sometimes as many as five. On busy days, he recalls that "I couldn't tell you, at 3:00 in the afternoon, what I played at 9:00 or 10:00 that morning."

Even the less-interesting sessions were a joy, in Marvin's view, because of the camaraderie. "Hangin' with these guys was like eating sugar all day." At least, that's what it was like for about the first 15 years that he spent as a studio player.

Over time, styles, preferences, and technologies changed and the writing became less jazz-influenced. By the early 1980s more studio work was being done with synthesizers and there were far fewer large-group sessions. In the aftermath of the 1981 Academy Award-winning movie *Chariots of Fire*, which won four awards including one for its soundtrack, the synthesizer and piano combination quickly became prominent in commercial recording. Many wind and string players found that their studio calls were substantially reduced, and it took years before these instruments gradually came back into fashion.

At the beginning of this period, the quality of ensemble writing declined as the prolific arrangers of previous decades exited the scene. Newcomers, many of them lacking large ensemble experience, initially failed to rise to the occasion. Some of them eventually learned what was needed and started to produce better quality work that Marvin enjoyed playing.

However, as the older players Marvin had worked with and learned from moved on, he began to feel that the "gentlemanliness" and "demeanor" of that generation were being lost. It wasn't just that the musicians no longer showed up at the studio wearing suits and ties. A new attitude was taking over in which the "we" community he felt connected to was being replaced by the "me" society – individuals who seemed to focus on themselves rather than seeking to be part of a sharing community. The changing behaviors and attitudes felt foreign to Marvin, and the overall experience became somewhat diminished. He continued doing studio work until 1990 as he looked for alternatives.

On the road again

Traditionally, there has been tension between studio players, who do most of their work for television, radio, movies, and advertising, and so-called "real" jazz players, who play clubs and concerts, record jazz albums, and go on the road. Even as young jazz fans in the 1970s, my friends and I sensed this tension among players that we admired on both sides. It seemed a bit pointless to us – like arguing about which supermodel is more attractive. However, it was all part of a larger, ongoing discussion about artistic value versus commercial success. Are these opposite ends of a spectrum? Can there be overlap without excessive compromise? How can individual artists balance these two factors?

A colleague who played on the jazz circuit told Marvin he was a good jazz player, but would never be a great jazz player until he got away from the routine of running from one studio gig to another, much of the time playing material unrelated to jazz that didn't include opportunities for improvisation. At the time, Marvin found this comment to be rather insulting. But later, after going back on the road as a soloist and with his own groups, he began to recognize the truth of that statement. While working in the studios, he felt pressure to focus as much on the hectic schedule of recording gigs as on the music itself. He didn't feel fully invested in the music because he saw it for the first time at the recording session, then never saw it again after the session was over. His job was to be a skilled craftsman, not an artist.

Though still successful in his studio work, Marvin gradually moved away from it starting around 1987 to become the "real" jazz player that he always wanted to be. It may seem unusual, or even unwise, to leave the relatively steady work in the studios and go back on the road, especially later in a musician's career, but Marvin wanted to seize the opportunity.

Career shifts in music, just like in other fields, can be hard. Marvin knew that this would mean reduced income and more travel. He could market his skills through his network of contacts, but this was the pre-Internet era, and most people didn't have email yet. So he acquired the most popular new communications tool of the time: a fax machine.

Marvin acknowledges that he hadn't been as diligent as he should have been at building and maintaining his contact list. He had to focus more on his communication skills, making phone calls and writing formal letters to feed into the fax machine. But only a small fraction of the recipients bothered to respond. This was a disappointing sign of the times to Marvin, who had always strived to provide timely responses to anyone who contacted him.

One of his key challenges was finding a good manager who could open doors that are often closed to artists who have not yet achieved recognition. Some managers only want to work with established artists who just need someone to handle their busy schedules and numerous contracts. They are hesitant to take on the hard work of building an emerging artist's career. Marvin was involved with two managers who were willing to put in the work and achieved some good results, but they were hampered by the fact that he was known as a studio musician rather than a jazz artist. It proved difficult to overcome that image even though his studio cred should have been seen as a strength.

But much can be achieved even in the absence of a manager. Eventually, people began to respond and the bookings started to grow. Jazz camps, clinics, workshops, and guest artist appearances had long been a part of Marvin's schedule. His involvement in jazz education had begun in 1960, the year before he finished college, and as he was leaving the studio scene 30 years later, it became a primary focus. Jazz education organizations and influential academics were an important part of his word-of-mouth network. He also attended conferences and performed as a guest artist across the United States and in Europe. Eventually, he built a schedule that kept him on the road about five months a year (cumulatively, made up of numerous short tours), allowing him to spend sufficient time at home with his family. There also were local gigs and rehearsal bands in the New York City area that expanded both the chances to play and the opportunities to meet new musical colleagues.

A lasting relationship with pianist Bill Mays began at rehearsals of Joe Rocisano's 13-piece band in 1995. This led to informal musical collaborations at Bill's house and quartet gigs with colleagues such as bassist Rufus Reid and drummer Ed Soph. Although his primary income came from the road gigs, Marvin enjoyed making music with friends on the New York scene, regardless of the money.

Marvin toured as a single artist, joining a variety of musical units for brief periods. He didn't try to start his own quartet or quintet and take it on the road for most of the year. That type of arrangement had become too difficult to maintain since its heyday a generation earlier. Travel had become more expensive, steady work was harder to come by, and musicians were more interested in pursuing multiple sources of creative stimulation – and income.

Being a single artist is nice work if you can get it, but it tends to be either feast or famine. You can be playing in top venues and working yourself to exhaustion for three months, then find yourself with little or no income for the next three months. Marvin lived in this world until he reached his late 70s and started to wind things down – just a couple of years before the coronavirus pandemic brought the music industry to a standstill. He feels great sympathy for early- and mid-career musicians who watched helplessly while concert tours got canceled and clubs closed – many of them permanently – leaving players with no income and substantially delaying their ability to pursue their musical goals.

That's not all, folks!

Marvin has shifted his efforts to nearby performances and recording projects with longtime colleagues such as pianist and composer/arranger

Mike Holober. The joy of the musical experience is still present, but he will be selective about his travel engagements. Colleagues still seek his talent, and he is happy to play whatever they have to offer him as long as it allows him to create good music and continue supporting younger players who are in their prime.

Although he has produced an enviable body of work as a solo artist, as an instrumentalist on a multitude of recordings, and as a sideman supporting a dazzling assortment of artists in concert, Marvin sets the standard for modesty. He believes that throughout his career, he was standing on the shoulders of those who came before him. He acknowledges that good fortune – despite occasional personal and professional setbacks – put him in the right place at the right time, and thankfully he was ready for it. His mantra was: show respect, have patience, learn from others. And then, when you're able, lend a hand to the next generation like the previous generation did for you.

Marvin didn't start his professional journey with a master plan, other than to have a successful career as an accomplished musician playing music that he loves. He didn't seek to become the most famous trumpeter in jazz by forming his own group, touring and recording endlessly, and trying to win fans away from Miles and Maynard. He aimed for more subtle contributions to the art, not for a big splash.

A story from his studio years illustrates his subtlety and modesty. In late 1970, Marvin was one of four trumpeters on an overdub recording session for an album. The other trumpeters were seasoned studio players Snooky Young, Mel Davis, and Ray Crisara. Horns and strings were being layered over the completed rhythm tracks. The project was Paul McCartney's *RAM* album, his second since the breakup of the Beatles. McCartney came to the trumpeters and said he had something he'd like one of them to do. Mel Davis immediately responded, "Let the kid do it" (referring to Marvin). The task was to play a flugelhorn solo to introduce the melody of the second half of "Uncle Albert/Admiral Halsey." When the song was released as a single in 1971, it went to number one on the *Billboard* Hot 100.

Fifty years later, Marvin's next-door neighbor was listening in her car to a satellite radio show that featured an interview with McCartney. After the host played "Uncle Albert/Admiral Halsey," McCartney said, "That was my old friend Marvin Stamm on flugelhorn."

Shocked when she heard this, the neighbor pulled off the highway and called Marvin. He was surprised to have been remembered, because his only conversation with McCartney was a few minutes of discussion on how the solo should sound. In general, Marvin remembers McCartney as a pleasure to work with, an artist who came to the studio prepared and knew what he wanted.

As a studio player, Marvin didn't receive any bonus when the tune became a huge hit. Nor was he credited in the liner notes when the album was released. It was indeed a subtle contribution, and one that he has never tried to overstate. But for a short time at the beginning of the 1970s, Marvin Stamm became the world's most famous unknown trumpeter.

Discography

Marvin Stamm has played trumpet and flugelhorn on thousands of recording projects and has performed with many notable jazz and pop artists. A partial list of these artists includes:
- Louie Bellson
- George Benson
- Paul Desmond
- Bill Evans
- Frank Foster
- Benny Goodman
- Lionel Hampton
- Woody Herman
- Freddie Hubbard
- Quincy Jones
- Thad Jones/Mel Lewis
- Stan Kenton
- Michel Legrand
- John Lewis
- Bob Mintzer
- Wes Montgomery
- Oliver Nelson
- Duke Pearson
- Frank Sinatra
- Stanley Turrentine

- Patrick Williams

The albums listed below are those on which Marvin is the leader, co-leader, or featured soloist.

1968 Machinations
1982 Stammpede
1990 Bop Boy
1993 Mystery Man
2000 By Ourselves
2000 The Stamm/Soph Project
2001 Elegance
2002 Ear Mix
2003 The Stamm/Soph Project – Live At Birdland
2006 Fast Track (Jack Cortner Big Band)
2006 The Nearness of You
2007 Alone Together
2007 Fantasy (Inventions Trio)
2008 Delaware River Suite (Inventions Trio)
2009 Sound Check (Jack Cortner Big Band)
2012 Life's a Movie (Inventions Trio)
2015 Balancing Act (Mike Holober's Balancing Act octet)
2019 Hiding Out (Gotham Jazz Orchestra)
2019 Live at Maureen's Jazz Cellar (Mike Holober Quartet)
2022 Don't Let Go (Mike Holober's Balancing Act octet)

Chapter 3

Holly Hofmann:
Shaping the Identity of Jazz Flute

Cleveland, Ohio in the mid-1970s offered a lot of opportunities to hear live jazz, both from touring artists who frequently came through town and from local talent. I was in college at the time, trying to attend as many of these events as I could. One of my favorite local groups was the very capable jazz ensemble at Case Western Reserve University, directed for part of that time by well-known composer-arranger Bob Curnow. A close friend of mine was playing first trombone in the band, so I tried to catch all of their concerts.

The ensemble did an impressive job for a college group that didn't include any music majors. Well, actually, there was one...

The band had made an unusual addition to the sax section. The normal complement of five players was supplemented by a woman playing flute. The first time I saw her, I didn't know for sure why she was there. Was there a special arrangement on the program that required this? Were none of the sax players able to double on flute?

As the concert got underway, the flutist seemed to be mostly doubling the lead alto parts, but eventually she got some solo space and delivered the best improvised choruses of the evening. Upon hearing this, I knew *exactly* why she was there.

Holly Hofmann with her husband, pianist Mike Wofford. (Photo credit: Beth Ross Buckley)

That was my first encounter with Holly Hofmann's playing. After college, I lost track of what she was doing until she started releasing her albums in the late 1980s, by which time she had relocated to San Diego. Her musical accomplishments since then have been remarkable, and her professional journey highlights the hard work and challenges of a life in jazz.

Holly was born and raised in the Cleveland area. Her father, a guitarist who owned a large jazz record collection, gave her early exposure to the jazz idiom. At age five, she began playing simple tunes on a flutophone to her father's accompaniment, then switched to recorder, and by age seven began her training on flute. She remembers her father's musician friends asking him why he started his daughter on a non-jazz instrument. This was an early portent of the artistic headwinds that Holly would encounter later.

Holly's parents recognized her aptitude and supported her interests, but insisted on strong classical training. For high school, she attended Interlochen Arts Academy in Michigan, after which she became a flute major at the Cleveland Institute of Music (which is affiliated with Case Western Reserve University). She studied with Maurice Sharp, who was the principle flutist with the Cleveland Orchestra for four decades. Sharp didn't want Holly to play jazz because he thought it would cause her to "develop bad habits," so her participation in the jazz ensemble was done without bothering to inform him.

One of Holly's fond memories from her first year of college was playing in the university's jazz ensemble at a festival where she had the opportunity to solo. Renowned trumpeter Clark Terry, who was at the festival and heard her play, later sought her out on the band's bus to offer encouragement: "Young lady, you keep going with this – you've got a thing!"

The next step for Holly was a master's degree program at the University of Northern Colorado, where she was granted a teaching assistantship. Despite receiving occasional positive reinforcement such as the compliment from Clark Terry, people were still telling Holly that she would never get work if she didn't double on sax, so she studied tenor sax along with her other graduate work. However, she found that it negatively affected the flute sound that she had carefully cultivated during her classical training, so she quickly gave it up. This reinforced her determination to make it as a jazz musician dedicated entirely to the flute.

Many sax players double on flute at varying levels of proficiency. But to Holly's trained ear, even with the most successful doublers, "You can always tell from their sound that it's not their first instrument." She found this to be true even with players as accomplished as reedman Frank Wess, one of her mentors, who was a pioneer in bringing flute into the big band setting during his time with Count Basie in the 1950s.

As a sax player who doubles on flute, I recognize that it would be unwise for me to try to impress Holly with anything I do on the instrument. Nonetheless, she has been a key role model in my study of flutology. She constantly demonstrates the importance of technical proficiency, and she never relies on the gimmicks used by many doublers, such as electronic enhancements or humming through the instrument. What comes out is great jazz – and I am sure that I'm not the only woodwind doubler who has noticed.

Early (legendary) mentors

During grad school, Holly had an opportunity that would be a dream come true for any informed student of jazz. (Alternatively, for the less courageous, it would be totally intimidating.) She spent the summers in New York studying with Frank Wess and composer-arranger-trombonist Slide Hampton, who took her to jam sessions and helped her expand her jazz repertoire and professional network.

Frank briefed Holly on how to prepare for the sessions, which involved knowing an extensive assortment of tunes, including bebop heads, and being able to play them in different keys, sometimes at breakneck tempos. He pushed her to practice with a metronome to keep driving her faster. He also made her aware that women instrumentalists typically were not invited to these sessions.

Jam sessions generally are perceived as something musicians do for fun or for practice. The variant known as a cutting session is highly competitive, the jazz equivalent of challenging others in the herd for the position of alpha male. Frank took Holly to sessions two or three times a week during those summer visits. She got accustomed to the other players looking askance at the five-foot-two girl who was invading their ranks.

Holly remembers that the other players "could be pretty brutal," and that more than one session left her crying. But she also remembers some guys who were "sweethearts."

Westward migration – Colorado to California

Many musicians find it necessary to work non-musical jobs for a while to make ends meet, and this was true for Holly. To supplement her musical income in Colorado, she took some jobs as a floral designer, a skill she had learned from her mother.

After working in Denver and Boulder for a while, Holly moved to San Diego in the mid-1980s when she was offered a position as a substitute in a band. As she built her connections and reputation in her new location, floral designing proved useful there as well.

Holly got to know Tom Burns, a Denver-based producer with Capri Records. Tom was a fan of her playing, but didn't offer her a recording deal until she moved to San Diego. Holly doesn't know why he waited so long, but it may have had something to do with getting her the right rhythm section. He told her that he would record her if she could get Mike Wofford on piano, Bob Magnusson on bass, and Sherman Ferguson on drums. The result was Holly's first two albums, *Take Note* (1988) and *Further Adventures* (1989). The first album had good sales and was getting some airplay, so Capri Records began receiving requests to book Holly's group at jazz festivals, starting with one in Clearwater, Florida, even before the second album was released. In the years that followed, she averaged about three months per year on the road until the coronavirus pandemic intervened in 2020.

One of the events Holly played in 1989, along with Mike Wofford on piano, was the wedding of saxophonist-flutist James Moody. The occasion drew several notable jazz colleagues, including trumpeter Dizzy Gillespie, who gave away the bride. After hearing Holly play, Diz asked her if she had listened to a lot of big band recordings. She told him about growing up hearing her father's huge record collection. He told her, "You don't sound like a flute player. You sound like a trumpet player." High praise indeed, considering the source. It has always been important to Holly to play her flute with the style and impact of a jazz horn, in the same vein as a trumpet or clarinet or sax, not just to provide a lilting obbligato to dress up an arrangement.

Holly later added alto flute to her musical arsenal, using it on an album for the first time in 2006 on three tracks of *Live at Athenaeum Jazz – Volume 2.* Her interest in playing it was encouraged by her colleague, flutist Ali Ryerson, who helped arrange for her to get an instrument from Sankyo. Later, in 2014, she recorded *Low Life* playing alto flute for the entire album. She started planning a sequel to *Low Life* in 2019, but when the pandemic came along she put the project on hold. Promoting an album means going on the road, and that wasn't going to happen for an extended period due to coronavirus concerns.

Collaborations

After her early recordings, Holly worked regular gigs around San Diego with Wofford and Magnusson. (Ferguson lived in Los Angeles, so they found local drummers for the quartet.) Starting in the early 1990s, she partnered with pianist Bill Cunliffe on several albums, and they toured internationally as a duo with appearances in Europe, Australia, and New Zealand. Cunliffe is equally accomplished in classical and jazz, so the two of them often combined elements of both in their performances, creating interpretations unlike any others in Holly's experience.

Bill Cunliffe, in Holly's view, has a rare gift for smoothly going back-and-forth between musical idioms. She remembers the remarkable way he demonstrated this ability during their tours. He would do a solo piece in which he would ask the audience to give him the names of three pieces of music: one popular, one classical, and one jazz. Then he would spontaneously weave them into a single piece containing elements of all of them. Mere mortals were left in awe at the satisfying results that Bill could produce after only a few moments of contemplation.

The mid-1990s marked the start of frequent collaborations with legendary bass player Ray Brown, including performances at Birdland, the Village Vanguard, and U.S. and European tours. He became a major influence on her career. He also had a nickname for her, calling her "Tales," which was a takeoff on the name of her 1995 album *Tales of Hofmann*, which itself was a play on the 19th century short stories and opera known as The Tales of Hoffmann. Often, when others heard him use this nickname, they didn't make these historical connections and thought he was calling her "Tails" based on unfounded assumptions about the nature of their relationship.

Holly saw each performance with Ray as a learning experience. It may not be immediately obvious what a bass player would teach a flute player, so I posed that question directly to Holly. She responded without hesitation that Ray shared his experience at creating set lists for concerts. This may seem like a very minor thing, especially coming from a bassist who most often performed with a trio, quartet, or quintet. Some groups that size just work off of a master list of prepared material and pick tunes on the fly after they're already onstage. But Ray had his own formula for setting the pace and keeping the audience interested.

For their appearances together, Ray made up a set list and asked Holly to do the same. In comparing the results, she asserts that Ray's lists were always more successful in terms of audience response, variations in pace and style, and changes in key. His formula, which left plenty of room for creative choices, worked like this:

- Start with something at a medium tempo that's easy and feels good. It can be a blues, but it doesn't have to be.
- The second piece should be a different groove, at a slightly different tempo. For example, a Latin tune.
- The third piece should be up-tempo – a barnburner that gets the audience's blood flowing.
- Next, change the timbre using duos within the quartet or quintet.
- Follow with a slow, lush ballad.
- Bring the tempo back up to medium-fast with a tune that the audience is likely to recognize.

Ray believed that audiences wanted to feel knowledgeable, and they wanted to be shown that the musicians can play. Therefore, each set should have at least two selections that the audience recognizes so they can make mental comparisons to other renditions they know, and thus be drawn into the immediate performance. Without this hook, listeners may not have a basis to judge the proficiency of the individual musicians, which may leave them less satisfied if the musicians are not already familiar to them.

Despite positive responses from his audiences, jazz critics sometimes complained that Ray Brown relied too much on standards and should have played more original material. Ray's retort: "If you're not playing for your audience, you might as well play in your garage."

Holly absorbed Ray's lessons on playlist planning and other aspects of performing. Another important lesson was that the audience in a concert hall with thousands of people should be treated just like a group of 25 guests you've invited to a concert in your home.

Of course, Holly's most important and lasting collaboration has been with Mike Wofford. It began when she moved to San Diego in the late 1980s. After many years of performing, recording, and booking concerts together, they became a married couple in 2000. ("It was like falling in love with my best friend.") Since then, Holly's musician friends have been jealous that she has a highly skilled live-in pianist.

But Mike is much more than that. He's a composer, arranger, and pianist who has performed and recorded with a who's who of jazz and pop artists. Many of his colleagues call him "the orchestrator" in tribute to both his arranging and the voicings he uses in his piano playing. A sample of his jazz experience includes work with saxophonists Stan Getz, Benny Golson, Joe Henderson, James Moody, Art Pepper, Sonny Stitt, Tom Scott, Bud Shank, Zoot Sims, and Phil Woods; trumpeters Chet Baker, Art Farmer, and Terell Stafford; trombonist Frank Rosolino; guitarists Kenny Burrell and Joe Pass; bassist Ray Brown; drummer Shelly Manne; and composer/bandleaders Benny Carter, Quincy

Jones, and Oliver Nelson. He also has served as conductor and pianist on concert tours with vocalists Sarah Vaughn and Ella Fitzgerald.

Drawing from that wealth of experience, Holly and Mike have worked together to craft their own interpretations of tunes from the jazz songbook with an appreciation for settings ranging from duos to big bands.

Preserving San Diego's jazz culture

For nearly the entire time she has been living in San Diego – except when performances were put on hold by the pandemic – Holly has been active in booking jazz series. When she arrived on the scene, the most prominent jazz club in San Diego, which attracted top talent from around the country, was Elario's, the 11th-floor restaurant at the Summerhouse Inn. By 1991, it was phasing out jazz, and after multiple ownership changes, jazz disappeared entirely by 1993. Holly was involved in projects that would help make up for the loss of the city's nationally recognized jazz venue. The first of these projects was located at the Horton Grand Hotel from 1991 to 1999. It was a Thursday-through-Saturday gig with the hotel providing rooms and food for visiting musicians. Mike was putting a lot of effort into booking the talent, but he asked Holly to take over when he got a call to go on the road with Ella Fitzgerald. She hadn't set out to be an event producer, but the experience taught her lessons that would prove useful.

"Everybody who was anybody played there," she recalls of the hotel series. Sometimes there were new artists who were on the verge of becoming prominent. Pianist and vocalist Diana Krall played one of her early gigs there, receiving $600 for her trio. Subsequently, her price doubled each year until the series could no longer afford her.

After the hotel series ended, Holly moved on to the San Diego Museum of Art and produced a jazz series there for eight years. The early-evening concerts were scheduled year-round for the first Wednesday of each month. They were held in the museum's auditorium, which seated about 450, and every show was a full house. Thanks to its reputation for quality, the series drew crowds regardless of the level of the artists' popularity.

Like the hotel series, the museum series was financially successful. In both cases, the end came when new management took over and decided to make a change.

There were similar efforts outside of San Diego as well. Holly worked on a summer series in the mid-2000s called Jazz in the City at the State Theater in New Brunswick, New Jersey. Also, she was the artistic director for the Oregon Coast Jazz Party from 2006-2019. The weekend event is held at the Oregon Coast Performing Arts Center west of Portland. Top-tier jazz artists show up individually – without their bands – and then form groups on the spot, resulting in spontaneous jams by improvisational masters. Kind of like an all-star game for jazz fans.

Holly believes it's important to get experienced musicians involved in booking events even though they usually are not fond of engaging in the business end of the music. Their utility in booking talent comes from knowing the needs of touring musicians as well as the music itself. They also know that you shouldn't put jazz in the wrong venues for the wrong reasons (e.g., nothing more than classy background music) because it won't make money. When that happens, jazz entertainment gets a reputation as a losing proposition.

Shaping young (and not-so-young) minds

Holly is an associate at the Young Lions Jazz Conservatory in San Diego, a nonprofit educational organization created and directed by trumpeter Gilbert Castellanos. It provides an immersive experience taught by professional jazz musicians for students ages 11-18. She also holds clinics at high schools and colleges on her road trips. She recognizes the lasting value of these programs, even knowing that most participating students will not seek music careers. But all of them can become the next generation of jazz listeners, enjoying lasting enrichment because they made music a key element in their lives.

Holly also is a faculty member for the Not-So-Young Lions classes for adults of all ages. Some of the participants are former musicians who want to get back into playing, and some are parents of the students in the Young Lions program who want to find out what jazz is all about, and why their kids love it so much. Often, adults can be great students because they are more motivated and disciplined. They don't have anyone forcing them to practice – they're doing it for the pure joy of the musical experience.

Holly finds that teaching jazz is "an interesting conundrum." Students need the right balance between learning chords and scales – which is necessary but not sufficient – and ear training. Improvisation, the heart of jazz, depends on developing an ear that can find a melodic path using chords and scales as the basis. Lack of adequate ear training tends to confine players to what is written in the chart, limiting their ability to spontaneously create their own melodies and embellishments. Regardless of their age, Holly likes to start students on manageable jazz elements like 12-bar blues, and she encourages them to listen to multiple renditions of jazz standards so they can hear how the great artists craft their own unique interpretations.

What's this? A female flutist from the San Diego?

There have been times when Holly has felt she had three strikes against her jazz career: she's a woman, a flutist, and she's not part of the New York jazz community.[†] Early on, she sensed the

---

[†] Academic researchers have found that variations of the "three strikes" metaphor are common among women in jazz. A prominent early example can be found in a 1951

need to be a leader, calling her own shots with her own groups, because there was — and to some extent, there still is — little acceptance of women as featured jazz instrumentalists. In her experience, bands rarely hire flute players and often don't want to hire women at all.

Ray Brown did his part to open the aperture for new approaches. Holly remembers that for her first European tour with his trio, the tour promoters had told Ray to bring along a tenor sax and a trumpet as guests. Instead, he brought Holly and violinist Regina Carter. "The promoters were just livid... there were some scenes when we were getting off the bus."

In media interviews, Holly often remarks that "If I had a dollar for every time I've been told that flute is not a jazz instrument, I would be wealthy and retired." Aside from Holly, only a few dedicated jazz flute players, such as Herbie Mann and Hubert Laws, have built a body of work that is widely recognized in American jazz circles. There have not been enough jazz flute recordings or concert appearances, in her estimation, to prompt audiences to develop an ear for it. She has always envisioned that she could be the one to change that, but so far she's not satisfied with the results. She

---

DownBeat article by well-known reviewer Leonard Feather about pianist Marian McPartland: "She is English, white, and a girl — three hopeless strikes against her."

still hears disparaging remarks indicating a lack of acceptance of the flute as a solo instrument in jazz.

Holly got another example of the flute's unfavorable status in 2019 when her agent was contacted by a jazz society on the East Coast that wanted to book the group, including Mike Wofford and trumpeter Terell Stafford, that had played on her 2010 album *Turn Signal*. They were ready to finalize the contract when the selection committee for the concert series asked them to eliminate the flute because they didn't think a flute player could be a headliner on a jazz event. Of course, none of the players would agree to this.

During my interviews with Holly, I was surprised to learn about how much resistance she has encountered to the concept of flute as a jazz horn. Many instruments, far less conventional than flute, have been used in jazz improvisation, including bass clarinet, double reeds, French horn, banjo, and harp. I've even heard an attempt to play jazz on bagpipes. (The less said about that, the better.) Jazz is a versatile idiom, and the acceptability of a particular instrument should depend on the skill with which it is played and the quality of the arrangements that employ it.

My own musical evolution, which took place almost entirely in large groups, occurred during a period in which doubling on clarinet almost disappeared as flute became the preferred double for saxophonists. There was never any doubt in my mind that flute is a jazz instrument, and I never heard any of my colleagues disparage it. As Peter

Westbrook stated in the conclusion of his extensive volume *The Flute in Jazz*:

> From a handful of performers in the 1950s we have seen an explosion in the use of the flute in jazz and all its various genres, both esoteric and commercial, both in the U.S. and abroad. The result is that there are far more flutists active in jazz than I ever anticipated.

He goes on to say that although the flute has not displaced the trumpet or saxophone in jazz, it has managed to carve out a major role for itself in a variety of settings.

Holly's quest to "make the flute just another jazz horn" may still be a journey in progress, but clearly there is some success. Cultural change takes a long time and the efforts of many, and Holly Hofmann has been a major player in shaping and accelerating that change.

References

Holly Hofmann is a Pearl Flutes artist and endorses Drelinger headjoints. Her website is https://www.hollyhofmann.com

Boomazian, Josiah, "Mary Lou Williams and the Role of Gender in Jazz," *Jazz Education in Research and Practice*, Vol. 3, No. 1, Winter 2022.

Levitan, Corey, "Elegy for Elario's: When the Jewel Ruled the Jazz," *La Jolla Light*, November 14, 2018 (https://www.lajollalight.com/art/music/sd-cm-ljl-elarios-20181102-htmlstory.html).

Van Vleet, Kaitlyn, "Women in Jazz Music: A Hundred Years of Gender Disparity in Jazz Study and Performance (1920-2020)," *Jazz Education in Research and Practice*, Vol. 2, No. 1, Spring 2021.

Westbrook, Peter, *The Flute in Jazz: Window on World Music*, Harmonia Books, 2011.

Discography

- 1988 Take Note!
- 1989 Further Adventures…
- 1992 Duo Personality
- 1995 Tales of Hofmann
- 1997 Just Duet
- 1998 Flutopia
- 1999 Live at Birdland
- 2003 Just Duet – Vol. 2
- 2003 Flutology: First Date
- 2003 Minor Miracle
- 2006 Live at Athenaeum Jazz – Vol. 2
- 2010 Three's Company
- 2010 Turn Signal
- 2012 Game Changer (with Ali Ryerson's Jazz Flute Big Band)
- 2014 Low Life

Chapter 4

Joe Eckert: To the Air Force and Beyond

I didn't have the opportunity to start studying music until I entered high school at age 13. I was surprised to find that the majority of the band's incoming freshmen already had been playing their instruments, or had taken piano lessons, for at least a couple of years. I couldn't even read music yet, so I had a lot of catching up to do.

A year later, after I had started to build up some confidence, a new kid arrived in the next freshman class who gave me even more catching up to do. He had been playing clarinet since he was six and alto and tenor saxes since he was 10. Joe Eckert had gotten his early start by inheriting the horns and receiving the encouragement of his older brother Bill. Joe became one of many people in my life who taught me a lesson applicable to music or any other endeavor: If you find yourself working alongside someone who is more capable and experienced, don't get frustrated or jealous or overcompetitive; learn from them, even if they're younger than you are. (I'm pretty sure that conveying this lesson was unintentional on Joe's part, and probably went unnoticed.)

Joe and I played side-by-side for the remainder of our high school time together, usually with him on alto and me on tenor, or both of us on clarinet.

That included marching band, concert band, clarinet quartet, jazz ensemble (which was still called "stage band" or "dance band" in those days), and the pit orchestra for the drama club's musicals.

Joe Eckert in a guest appearance with the Airmen of Note after his retirement from the Air Force.
(Photo credit: U.S. Air Force Band)

Everybody knew that Joe would embark on an active music career, and this was reinforced by his subsequent entry into the music conservatory at nearby Baldwin-Wallace College (now Baldwin Wallace University). What we couldn't have known at that time was that a major highlight of his career would be 20 years as the lead alto saxophonist (including six years as music director) of the U.S. Air Force Airmen of Note, the service's premier jazz ensemble.

From academia to military life

Joe left our home town of Cleveland, Ohio in 1977 to study at the University of North Texas, and married his college sweetheart Jackie a year later. In high school and college, he had been a big fish in a small pond (musically speaking), but then as a graduate student he became a newcomer in a nationally recognized jazz program with 120 sax players. Getting picked for the first-chair position was no longer assured.

The North Texas jazz program names its ensembles after the hour at which each group rehearses. The One O'Clock Lab Band is touted as the premier ensemble, and it has recorded an album annually since 1967. Joe was in the Two O'Clock band until his final year when he moved up to the top band during the last year it was directed by Leon Breeden. That year, the band performed at a jazz festival in Interlochen, Switzerland. During their two-week stay, they only played four concerts – a very light workload. But in such a nice setting, no one was complaining, and some of the players saw it as more of a vacation for outgoing director Breeden and his wife.

Joe recalls a sightseeing excursion that involved a rather rugged climb to a hilltop café with two other band members. They were proud of themselves for making it to the top, but one of them – future trombone star Conrad Herwig – broke his ankle on the way down.

Joe received his master's degree in 1979 and stayed at North Texas, taking courses toward a Doctor of Musical Arts degree, until his fellowship ran out in 1981. After interviewing at universities in Colorado, Iowa, and Missouri, Joe landed at West Virginia University, where he was Assistant Band Director and Saxophone Instructor from 1981 to 1984. Organizationally, this gave him a role in the marching and concert bands, but he focused his efforts on building a jazz program and teaching his sax students.

Although he enjoyed teaching, he didn't want it to displace his own performing. During his years in college and grad school, he had enjoyed a busy playing schedule of rehearsals, gigs, recording sessions, and even some jam sessions. For a jazz saxophonist, those opportunities were scarce in and around Morgantown, so he had to drive 75 miles to play in Pittsburgh. There he was able to hook up with the house band at a hotel called the Holiday House which frequently supported shows by touring artists. The band was directed by Randy Purcell, a trombonist who had formerly played with Maynard Ferguson's band. It was good work, but Joe missed the type of challenging playing he had experienced in the One O'Clock band at North Texas.

In 1984, he saw an ad in *The International Musician*, the newspaper of the musicians union. The Airmen of Note jazz ensemble was looking for a sax player. Joe was well aware of the reputation and caliber of the Note (as well as other U.S. military jazz groups) and saw the potential for more challenging work. He wondered if the position would be filled before he could get his application submitted, and how many other players around the country would be vying for this slot. He also had to convince his wife that becoming a military family would be a good move. By this time, he and Jackie had a daughter.‡

The job was still open, so he set up his audition. He later found out that the Note had heard 35 other candidates before him, so it was remarkable that Joe was offered the job on the same day he gave a very thorough and tiring audition.

The audition was an elaborate hour-long process that involved the whole band. It included improvised solos, sight-reading of charts with demanding sax section parts, and doubling on clarinet, flute, and even a bit of piccolo. Then he played quartet-style with the rhythm section.

---

‡ Fast forward to today: Their daughter Elizabeth is a singer on two albums under the name Bourbon & Bliss. Their son Alan, born in 1986, is a talented drummer.

Looking back on it, he calls the audition "a great experience."

Once a musician is accepted into a military band, they get a contract that stipulates that they will have a permanent duty assignment in a particular unit, such as the Air Force bands based in Washington, DC. The musician then takes this contract to a recruiting center to begin the induction process without having to go through an assessment to determine an appropriate assignment. Most people are unaware of this special handling of musical recruits. Throughout their service, military musicians are routinely confronted with questions from family, friends, and audience members who ask things like, "What do you do in your regular duties? Fly airplanes?" In reply, they reveal the shocking truth: "No, we're real, full-time, professional musicians."

Basic training for an "old" musician

As an incoming musician, Joe had the choice of doing the regular basic training or being in the drum & bugle corps. (Later, it became customary for all musicians to do drum & bugle corps rather than having a choice.) The latter choice would have taken longer because of a later start date, and Joe would have had to play percussion because drum & bugle corps don't have woodwinds. So he chose basic training, which was held in San Antonio during the opening weeks of the Texas summer.

At 27, Joe was older than the rest of the recruits, who were mostly around 18. They arrived at the training camp at 11:00 pm and it was clear they wouldn't be getting much sleep on that first night. Their indoctrination into herd mentality began immediately. They were taken to their barracks, and after getting their bunk assignments and their first dose of the sergeant's verbal assertiveness, they were told it was time to eat even though it was well after midnight. When the meal was finished, everyone was required to shower and shave, and the sergeant made clear that "I don't want to see any hair on your face!" One young recruit took this quite literally and shaved off his eyebrows.

Lights out came at 2:30 am with a wake-up call set for 5:00 am. Thus began six weeks of character building in the U.S. military's version of on-the-job training, with rewarding experiences like running in combat boots. Throughout that time, Joe kept quiet about his status as a musician. It didn't seem like a good idea to let the drill sergeants know that once the training was over, he would outrank them.

Performances and tours

Joe was glad to finally get to Washington and hook up with the Note at its headquarters at Bolling Air Force Base (now Joint Base Anacostia-Bolling). His first gig was a celebration for World War II veterans, an annual event at that time. Many of the veterans were still around and able to attend in 1984, including many members of the Glenn Miller band, such as drummer Ray

McKinley and clarinetist Peanuts Hucko, as well as singing groups The Modernaires and The Four Freshmen. The band was set up in an airplane hangar and they were wearing World War II-era Army Air Corps uniforms. Joe didn't know what kind of crowd to expect, so he was taken by surprise when the hangar doors opened and in came 25,000 people. Not bad for his first gig with a band that would be his home as lead alto player for the next 20 years.

A short time later, the Note played a concert at Constitution Hall in DC. The show featured guest vocalist Carmen McRae, who was a heavy smoker. Before going onstage, she was craving a cigarette and didn't have one, so a trumpet player offered her one of his smokes. The cigarette had no filter, which may have made it too potent for the singer. Joe's most vivid memory of the concert was the coughing fit she had, lasting a few minutes, when she started to sing her first tune.

The band practiced three days a week in the afternoons, and the performances typically were on weekends. Initially, that was the extent of the duty schedule, which Joe found a bit dull even though he loved playing with such an outstanding band. As he took on more responsibilities over the years, things got much busier and it became a 40-hour week and more.

The band went on two or three public relations tours per year (depending on budgets), totaling about 60 days on the road. The Army, Navy, and Air Force bands toured the country on a rotation that would give each service's groups exposure in all regions of the country every few years.

There were occasional short-notice calls from higher officials to perform for government functions, but not typically from the White House because those events usually went to the Marine Band ("The President's Own"). That changed when Bill Clinton's White House began specifically requesting the Note. Knowing that Clinton was a sax player, the director thought it would be amusing to bring an extra tenor sax to one of the White House gigs. It was placed on a stand at the front of the stage and they called it "The 1st Tenor."

On one occasion, President Clinton came over to talk to the band and asked if he could play a solo on one tune. It's very difficult for a service member to say no to the commander-in-chief, so the president got his solo. He was clearly having a good time with the band, which caused him to ignore the tightly choreographed schedule that spelled out minute-by-minute when he was supposed to be greeting guests, talking to specific dignitaries, giving a speech, or otherwise mingling with the attendees. His staffers were constantly looking at their watches and trying to redirect him away from the stage.

One of the challenges of playing at the White House is the unpredictability of the timing. The band would be set up in the East Room, but would have to wait in a basement room until they were called to perform. They never knew how long their wait would be. It could be a half-hour, or it could be two hours, making it difficult to be warmed up and ready to play when the time finally came. But the reward was that after the event, the band was invited to partake of the leftover food that had been laid out for the guests.

For events at secure locations like the White House and the Pentagon, the musicians had to go through a variety of security checks – opening their instrument cases for inspection, being probed by bomb-sniffing dogs, etc. – even though they all had security clearances. The guests at the events, who may or may not have had clearances, didn't undergo the same scrutiny, and there were times at the Pentagon when pizza delivery guys walked right past them and into the building. Of course, all this changed after the attacks of September 11, 2001, when security procedures tightened up for everybody.

By the early 1990s, Joe was involved in the planning and execution of tours and concerts, some of which included guest artists. This led to the establishment in 1990 of the Note's long-running Jazz Heritage Series, which brings top jazz artists to the Washington, DC area for free concerts. A typical season includes one concert each month in February, March, and April, each with a different guest artist. Having attended many of these concerts, featuring award-winning artists such as Al Jarreau, Phil Woods, and Christian McBride, I can verify that they are textbook examples of the versatility and impact of a large, well-rehearsed jazz ensemble.

The Note's 40th anniversary concert in 1990 at the Kennedy Center featured singer Toni Tennille, whose father had been a big band musician. She came to the event with her own big band charts, arranged by renowned composer/arranger Sammy Nestico. The band invited Sammy, who had written for and played with the Note years earlier, to be the guest conductor.

The Air Force Band program had been holding an annual composition competition named after Colonel George Howard, its first commander (1947-63). That gave Joe the idea that the Note should have its own jazz composition competition, named after Sammy Nestico. He contacted Sammy, who was thrilled and honored by the idea. The first Nestico award was presented at a jazz educators conference in Anaheim, California in 1995.

Joe was the Note's music director from 1998 until his retirement from the Air Force in 2004. One of the band's big projects during that time was a celebration of Duke Ellington's 100th birthday that included performances and recordings of all of Duke's symphonic works.

Drummer Harold Jones was a guest performer with the Note around this time. He is best known for his work with Tony Bennett and for a productive five-year stint with the Count Basie band. One of the 15 albums he recorded with Basie was the collection of Sammy Nestico charts called *Basie, Straight Ahead*, which is well known to generations of big band players. Joe produced a concert, held at George Mason University near DC, in which Jones joined the Note in presenting all the tunes from that classic album.

Sometimes, guest artists tried to test the band in odd ways. Joe recalls a concert featuring trumpeter Jon Faddis, and particularly one of his charts that called for repeated full-band punches at the end. At rehearsal, the band wanted to know how many times the punch figure would be repeated, and Faddis told them he would signal them at the performance. When the time came in the concert, Faddis turned to the band and said, "57." Fortunately, everyone in the band knew how to count that high, so they managed to end the tune together.

There were many occasions when the Note played at jazz festivals and were joined for impromptu performances by respected artists who were also on the festival program. The band members always were thrilled at the opportunity to play with well-known recording artists. But those artists probably were just as thrilled to play in front of a band with the competence and reputation of the Note.

Performing abroad

Among the highlights of Joe's overseas trips with the Note were two South American tours in 1989 (two weeks in Brazil) and 1990 (one month traveling through Brazil, Uruguay, Argentina, Chile and Panama). The latter featured the "Serenade in Blue" show that included a string section and singers.

The goodwill tours were part of an effort to cement relations among the U.S. Air Force and its counterparts in South American countries, which may have helped when the military coalition for the 1991 Iraq war was formed. The performers got a warm reception wherever they went. Activities included combined performances with host military organizations as well as with local musicians.

Exposure to Latin music as played by the local musicians was eye-opening. Most jazz musicians in the United States have plenty of experience playing Latin-style tunes, but as Joe found out, "We all think we know how it goes, but we don't." For example, the percussion patterns that we think are two-bar repeats are actually more complex and may be eight-bar patterns.

In Brazil, Joe got to see where the "Girl from Ipanema" walked, and as the song requires, he said "Ahhh..." While seeing the sights and traveling to gigs, he was glad that others were doing the driving. He observed what many travelers to Latin America have commented on: traffic signs and signals are treated as merely suggestions. Combine that with narrow streets and aggressive drivers and you have a situation in which it seems best to just close your eyes until you reach your destination.

One of the performances in Brazil was at an orphanage, which was a bittersweet experience. The kids were great – they were friendly and they loved the music. But as they crowded around the band members, they tugged on their shirtsleeves and begged them, in their best broken English, to please adopt them and take them home. Joe and his bandmates found it hard to observe so much need but feel so powerless to do anything about it.

Moving on to Uruguay, Joe had an unpleasant reaction when he drank some water or ate something that set off a major international incident in his gastrointestinal tract. (Some of the band members chose to avoid this problem by drinking only alcoholic beverages.) It flared up during the first half of a performance, so Joe sought help from the tour's medical officer during intermission. "I'm not going to make it through the second half," he told the medic. "Do you have anything that can help me?" The medic gave him a vial of an unidentified yellow liquid, "the most foul-tasting stuff I ever drank in my life," which did the trick and cleaned him out for the next three days.

The Chilean air force put on an air show just for the tour members, doing precision flying similar to the U.S. Air Force Thunderbirds, but with propeller-driven aircraft. At the end of the show, the pilots hopped out of their cockpits in their goggles and scarves, looking much like Snoopy in his dogfights with the Red Baron.

In Panama, the group stayed at a Marriott hotel that still had bullet holes from the siege to capture the dictator Manuel Noriega a few months earlier. At this stage of the trip, Joe was designated as the "bag man" who had to account for all baggage as the group prepared to return home. Every instrument case and piece of luggage was opened and inspected by Panamanian authorities. Of course, the travelers had picked up a lot of souvenirs along the way, including many bottles of wine and other spirits. All of these got confiscated – but not because they were illegal. The local customs officials must have had quite a party that night.

Another memorable international excursion was a 10-day tour of Europe and the Middle East in 2002. The transportation was a C-141 cargo plane, designed for extreme comfort if you happen to be a shipping container. If you're human cargo, you get to sit around the perimeter of the cargo bay enjoying the nonstop vibration and noise that take the place of an inflight movie to help pass the time.

The nine-hour flight from Andrews AFB near DC to Ramstein Air Base in Germany arrived at its destination at about 10:00 am local time. Despite the difficulty of getting any sleep on the flight, the band immediately had to go into rehearsal for a performance that evening.

After a couple of shows on military bases there, it was time to head to the Middle East. The performers visited Bahrain, Kuwait, Qatar, Turkey, and the United Arab Emirates. It was a fast-paced tour, at one point presenting three shows in three different countries in one day. Their audiences were deployed personnel at military facilities. Unlike in South America, they didn't go out and perform in the local communities, although they did sample some of the local hospitality in

Turkey. On the way home there was a stop to perform at Aviano Air Base in Italy, topped off by the best multi-course meal that country has to offer.

Maintaining support for military bands

In 1990, in between the two South America tours, the Air Force bands were facing a possible 10 percent budget cut that included a proposal to shrink the Note to a 10-piece show band. The horns would be reduced to two saxes, two trumpets, and one trombone – an existential threat to the band's cultural heritage, its relevance on the American jazz scene, and possibly to Joe's career. As a precaution, he auditioned for the Marine Band in case his position got cut. But that wasn't the only response from Joe and his fellow bandsmen. It was time to bring out the big guns.

The Note had performed with famed *Tonight Show* bandleader and trumpeter Doc Severinsen, who was at the height of his popularity at the time. Additionally, Doc's arranger/saxophonist Tommy Newsom was an alumnus of the Note. Both of them endorsed full funding for the band with a plea for support to the national audience of the *Tonight Show*. (At the time, another lower-key late-night talk show followed the *Tonight Show*, and Joe called in to discuss the band's dilemma with host Tom Snyder.) This coincided with a letter, signed by Doc, that was published as a full-page ad in the music educators' publication *The Instrumentalist*. Under the heading "Save the Airmen of Note – An

Urgent Letter from Doc Severinsen," it said, in part:

> The Airmen of Note, one of the finest big bands in the world, is in a precarious position due to cutbacks in the military... I have performed with this great band on numerous occasions.
> The Air Force has decided that, as of September 1992, the Airmen of Note will suffer a cut of eight members, reducing the band from a full 18-piece big band to a 10-piece group. This drastic, unprecedented assault on one of the few truly professional big bands must not be taken lightly in this time of widespread cuts in the arts.

The letter ended with a request for readers to write or call their congressmember and the Secretary of the Air Force. Apparently, many readers – and *Tonight Show* viewers – did so. The Air Force was inundated with calls objecting to the budget cut, and as a result the word came down from the highest level of the service that the reduction would not happen. The band's fate was resolved by Memorial Day of that year, at which time the Note played a concert in DC featuring their close ally, Doc Severinsen.

This 1990 incident was not the first time that U.S. military band programs have faced the possibility of devastating budget cuts, nor would it be the last. (For example, another effort to enact major cutbacks took place in the House of Representatives in 2011, but it was not taken up by the Senate.) Critics from across the political spectrum see military music as a non-essential activity that could be eliminated to trim the Defense Department's huge budget. These are purely symbolic actions that would allow congressional appropriators and other officials to say they are trimming the fat from the Pentagon's budget. Reductions of actual significance are much more difficult to achieve, and any cuts to the military music program couldn't make a noticeable dent in overall spending. The total defense budget for fiscal year 2021 was over $700 billion, with the Department of the Air Force (including the Space Force) accounting for $204 billion. The total amount spent on all of the 100-plus national and regional military bands across all of the armed services was in the neighborhood of $300 *million*, which sounds like a lot of money but is a microscopic fraction of one percent of the defense budget. And the Airmen of Note get just a tiny portion of that.

 U.S. military bands are a tradition that goes back to Revolutionary War times, but there are more reasons to keep them around than just tradition. They provide the musical accompaniment at many types of ceremonial occasions, such as visits by heads of state, promotion and change-of-command ceremonies, ship christenings, and military funerals. They are powerful public relations assets both at home and abroad. They also help improve morale by entertaining military personnel deployed around the world.

Skeptics of the value of live music may feel that it could simply stop being offered at these events. (Although they probably wouldn't want to be the ones to tell deployed forces that all they're going to get is a disc jockey.) However, our military allies will continue doing it, so it won't be long before senior officials start asking, "Why can't we have live ceremonial music like these other countries do?"

Hiring private-sector musicians instead of using military personnel may seem like a viable alternative, but I'm not aware of any study on whether or not that would save money. A commercial approach is unlikely to produce a dedicated cadre of on-call musicians over which the military can enforce quality control and responsive scheduling.

Maybe the solution is to take the opponents of military bands to some concerts. At least some of them will come out singing a different tune.

Life outside The Note

Teaching has been an enduring aspect of Joe's musical career. During his time with the Note, the band established a jazz outreach program to connect with schools in the DC area as well as those along the route of their tours. But that wasn't the only pedagogical aspect of Joe's professional efforts.

When he left academia to join the Air Force, Joe was happy to get away from university bureaucracy (which at times can be even more imposing than in the government) but he came to miss the interaction with students. He also feels that teaching can make you a better player because you're forced to analyze what you do so you can convey it to others. To reconnect with the positive aspects of teaching, he got back into it while he was still early in his Air Force career.

Joe felt like he was "leading a double life" during his time in the Washington, DC area. In addition to his work with the Note, in 1987 he was offered a part-time teaching position at Shenandoah University in Winchester, Virginia – 87 miles away from his Air Force job. This made for some long days and a lot of driving. The action started before 7:00 in the morning and continued until 9:00 or 10:00 at night, putting 425,000 miles on his Plymouth Colt.

He put on some more miles (although not in his car) when Shenandoah's jazz ensemble got the opportunity to visit China in 1993, and he took leave from the Note to go with them. They flew into Hong Kong (still a U.K. territory at the time) and from there to Nanchang on the mainland. Facilities at the airport were quite rustic at the time, and the 1400 km train ride to Beijing, notably deficient in modern amenities, took 32 hours.

The band members enjoyed their performances and their interactions with the Chinese students.

Before they left there was a big "family style" dinner. One of the unusual features was a big bowl of soup in the middle of the table with something floating in it – a chicken head. Tradition dictated that the honored guest should take the chicken head and suck out its brains, which are considered to be a delicacy. All of the students and their chaperons looked around at each other reluctantly until the eldest member of the group (not Joe) embraced the offering.

After a week in China, the band had a layover in Hawaii on the way home. Joe arranged for Jackie and the kids to join him for that last stop on the trip. After they got there, the jazz ensemble's gig got canceled, so they found themselves stuck in Hawaii for six days with nothing to do but try to enjoy themselves. What a tough break.

Joe's demanding schedule and long commute lasted 17 years, the remainder of his time in the Air Force. After that, he became a full-time professor at Shenandoah and took over as director of the university's jazz ensemble, a position that he retained for three years. During his tenure, the ensemble was featured at jazz festivals at North Texas and Notre Dame, recorded two albums, and hosted several guest artists including saxophonist Bob Mintzer, trumpeters Marvin Stamm and Jon Faddis, trombonist John Fedchock, and drummer Duffy Jackson.

Joe was playing a few gigs around DC and Baltimore, but he was largely absent from the area's freelance work for many years due to his packed schedule. He felt some withdrawal symptoms after retiring from the Air Force because he missed the playing he had done with the Note.

In 2007, former North Texas colleague Gary Whitman contacted Joe about a position that had opened at Texas Christian University in Fort Worth. It was considered an entry-level (assistant professor) job, so Whitman wasn't sure the pay would be adequate for someone like Joe, who had over two decades of university teaching experience. As it turned out, the pay was better than the full professor position that Joe held at Shenandoah – and there would be plenty of performing opportunities.

Joe focused on building the saxophone program when he arrived at TCU. Four years later, the Director of Jazz Studies retired and he was tapped to take over that role. Throughout his tenure, he has performed many faculty recitals and has been a frequent guest soloist, clinician, and adjudicator at a variety of college and high school jazz festivals in the region.

The TCU jazz program has been hosting its own jazz festivals every year since 1978 (except during the pandemic). The festival participants are local and out-of-state high schools, and the music faculty also present a concert. The festival ends with the university's jazz ensemble performing with a prominent guest artist. Joe has been able to call on his experience and connections gained during his years with the Note to attract performers such as John Fedchock, Duffy Jackson, trumpeter Randy Brecker, and bassist Rufus Reid.

At one of the festivals, there were some worrisome moments during preparations for a guest appearance by organist Joey DeFrancesco. The concert hall set up a Hammond B3 organ for him, but when he tried it out, he pressed one key and all of the power in the hall went out. Fortunately, electrical repairs were completed in time to present a successful concert.

In addition to holding its own festivals, the TCU jazz ensemble, under Joe's direction, has been an active participant in many regional and national jazz festivals. The group was poised to go international in 2020, when they were invited to perform at the prestigious Montreux Jazz Festival in Switzerland, a two-week gathering that typically draws around 250,000 people. It was to be held in July of that year, but unfortunately it was canceled for the first time since its inception in 1967 due to the coronavirus pandemic. The festival organizers extended invitations to all of the scheduled performers to participate in the next year's event, but by summer 2021 TCU still was not allowing international travel, much to the disappointment of the student musicians.

Outside the university, the Dallas-Fort Worth area has offered many performing opportunities. Gary Whitman, who alerted Joe to the TCU job, was the bass clarinetist with the Fort Worth Symphony. After Joe came to TCU, Whitman got his name on the call-up list as a substitute when the orchestra needed a woodwind player, and eventually he became their first-call saxophonist.

The Fort Worth Symphony members play more than just classical music concerts. They often support the local performances of touring shows, including Broadway musicals. Joe has played sax and woodwind doubles in pit orchestras for a number of these shows, such as *West Side Story* and *Annie*, as well as some in Dallas including *Porgy & Bess* and *Chicago*.

In September 2015, Doc Severinsen was a guest soloist with the Symphony. He brought his own arrangements, and Joe was set to play alto sax and clarinet. During preparations, he was asked if he would be willing to play flute on one tune, which included an extended improvised flute solo. None of the orchestra's flute players wanted to do it. Doc told Joe to come up front for that tune, making it the first time that he was standing in front of the Fort Worth Symphony as a featured soloist. He never imagined that this occasion would have him playing flute instead of sax, standing next to Doc Severinsen. (Joe's wife Jackie attended the concert. Afterwards, she said to him, "I didn't know you could do that!")

The next chapter

It's been said that if you truly enjoy what you're doing throughout your career, then you never actually "work" a day in your life. In that sense, Joe Eckert has never "worked" – he has pursued his passion, unwaveringly, giving it all the time and effort it has required of him. It hasn't always been easy (although he often makes it look that way) because there have been some disruptive life changes along the path. But Joe aimed for an impactful music career that touched a lot of lives, and he seems to have achieved it.

There will be more performances, more teaching, and maybe some new ways of making a difference in the jazz community. So stay tuned – Joe's not done.

References

Reuters News Service, "Montreux Jazz Festival cancelled for first time in its history," April 17, 2020 (https://www.reuters.com/article/us-music-jazz-montreux/montreux-jazz-festival-cancelled-for-first-time-in-its-history-idUSKBN21Z14S).

Texas Christian University Jazz Festival (https://finearts.tcu.edu/music/events-and-programs/festivals/jazz-festival/)

University of North Texas One O'Clock Lab Band (https://oneoclock.unt.edu)

U.S Air Force Airmen of Note (https://www.music.af.mil/Bands/The-United-States-Air-Force-Band/Ensembles/Airmen-of-Note/)

Discography

With the Airmen of Note:
    1985 Crystal Gardens
    1988 Somewhere Out There
    1990 Jazz Heritage
    1991 Santa Claus is Comin' to Town

1993 Children of the Night
1994 The Glenn Miller Tradition
1996 Blues & Beyond
1997 Legacy
1998 Christmas Time is Here
1998 Reeds and Rhythm
1998 Remembering the Glenn Miller Army Air Forces Orchestra
1999 Duke Ellington Symphonic Portrait (w/USAF Orchestra)
1999 Invitation
2000 Let's Dance
2000 Fifty Years of the Airmen of Note
2004 iTiempo Latino – A Celebration of Latin Jazz
2010 60 Years of the Airmen of Note

With other artists:
1976 Wild Cherry
1981 University of North Texas One O'Clock Lab Band
1994 Forced Air Heat (Bruce Gates Jazz Consortium Big Band)
1995 Joyous Reunion (Bruce Gates Jazz Consortium Big Band)
2005 Scat Like That (children's album by Cathy Fink & Marcy Marxer, arrangements by Mike Crotty; winner of a Grammy Award for best Children's album)
2012 A Drop of Romance (Bourbon & Bliss)
2014 The Trouble We Crave (Bourbon & Bliss)
2018 Pictures at an Exhibition (Fort Worth Symphony Orchestra)

Chapter 5

Encounters with Jazz Influencers

One of the recurring themes in these chapters is jazz education. All of the musicians profiled here have been involved in creating a path to musical fulfillment for new generations of players and listeners. They are a small sample of the countless teachers and role models who inspire passion for music, from in-person instructors who give lessons and direct school bands to recording artists who teach us from afar without even knowing it. For me, the list of influencers is very long and includes far more than just my co-instrumentalists. One of the important lessons in an individual's jazz evolution is that every encounter with an accomplished artist is a learning experience, regardless of whether they are older or younger, a horn player or a rhythm player, a bandleader or a writer.

Influential writers deserve special mention because often we take them for granted. We buy some music, or someone sets it on the stand in front of us, and we just focus on the execution without considering what went into the creation of that music. Or how much it will affect who we become as musicians.

Inspiration comes from many directions and begins early. Before I started studying music or building my record collection, I listened to 1960s Top 40 radio and my mother's collection of old big band records. Adding to that mix were sounds as varied as Henry Mancini scores for movies and television, and the pop recordings of groups such as the Beatles and Herb Alpert & the Tijuana Brass. (Yes, the latter was very commercial, but my reaction was: "Oh cool – horns!")

The very long list of composers and arrangers who have shaped students of jazz for decades deserve their own book, so I'll simply highlight two that I have found highly inspiring. Sammy Nestico taught multiple generations of players what a jazz ensemble chart should look like and what a modern big band should sound like. He did this by giving us hundreds of arrangements that please the ear and are fun to play, and therefore have become our textbook. His work is represented in music libraries from high school and college bands to top-tier groups like Count Basie and the Airmen of Note. It will continue to be heard for generations to come.

Similarly, Lennie Niehaus produced an abundance of big band charts, most prominently for Stan Kenton, and then moved on to a long career writing for television and movies. Less obvious but still highly influential was his output for small ensembles (such as sax quartet) and his method books and etudes that help students develop their jazz style.

I never got to personally thank Sammy or Lennie for all they did to help me develop my playing and writing. But I did have in-person experiences with some other key influencers.

Lessons from "The Old Man"

My first jazz teacher was Jim Anastasi, who offered all the encouragement and enthusiasm a student could hope for. His day job was testing horns at King Musical Instruments in Eastlake, Ohio, a position he held for almost four decades. But in the evenings and on Saturdays, he gave lessons on trumpet and trombone. When I studied valve trombone with him in the mid-1970s, he encouraged his students (which included my brother and some of our friends) to refer to him as "the Old Man." That seems funny now, because at the time he was about 50.

Like many brass teachers, Jim worked us through *Arban's Complete Conservatory Method* to ensure we had proper classical training. But he always set aside some time at the end of each lesson to develop our jazz chops. Each week, he would write out the melody of a tune, starting with "Satin Doll" and "Over the Rainbow" and continuing with his favorite jazz standards. Our homework would be to play with it, embellish it, and then come back the next week to render our own interpretation for him.

The jazz training wasn't confined to the weekly lessons. In addition to recommending artists and albums, the Old Man would occasionally invite us to his house for a listening session, preceded by an excellent Italian dinner prepared by his wife. As young men sometimes do, we gorged ourselves on the great food until we could barely get up from the dining table. As we settled into the living room and Jim started choosing some records to play, he would turn to us and ask, "You cats want some Jello?"

Jim was a diehard fan of Maynard Ferguson, so we sampled a lot of the great trumpeter's work, especially from the 1950s and early 60s. He treated us to a running commentary, making sure we understood that Maynard was not a "screech" trumpeter, but a true jazz soloist. "Listen to the ideas that cat is playing!" he would say.

There was storytelling as well. The anecdote I remember best is about his experience in the U.S. Army band during the last couple of years of World War II. Jim was playing fourth trumpet in a big band that was touring military bases on the home front. The Army decided to form a second band that would entertain troops deployed overseas. Jim became the lead trumpeter for the U.S.-based band as many of his colleagues got transferred to the new group. He never told us exactly what happened next – perhaps the details were never fully known – he simply said that the band that went to Europe never came back. He concluded the story by saying, "And that's how music saved my life."

On one occasion, Jim invited us to join him at Cleveland's Aragon Ballroom for a performance by trumpeter Harry James and his band. The Aragon was like a time machine back to the 1930s, with its

Art Deco design and swing era music. (It continued to feature swing dancing until 1989.) That night in the mid-1970s, we behaved just like the band's fans did in the old days. We gathered around the stage, watching and listening to the band, oblivious to the dancers. And we weren't the only ones – we were just a small part of the crowd of fans.

In the midst of that crowd, we struck up a conversation with a guy who seemed to be much younger than the average attendees. He turned out to be Mike Vax, who had recently been Stan Kenton's lead trumpeter. Since he wasn't playing in the band, we asked the obvious question, "What brings you here?" He replied that he was traveling through the area and stopped in to see his friend and fellow Kenton alum Quinn Davis, who was playing lead alto sax that night.

The Old Man's students greatly appreciated all the things he did for them beyond the weekly lessons to further their jazz education, like introducing us to great players and teaching us about the artists and their history. And if we wanted to buy a horn from King Instruments, he would personally choose it for us (in my case, a King 3B valve trombone, and for my brother, a Silver Flair trumpet). We owe him a lot for lessons that have lasted a lifetime. Unfortunately, I missed the opportunity to interview him for this book. The unforgettable Jim Anastasi passed away in April 2021 at the age of 95. He had literally become the Old Man, a label still used with respect and affection.

On the road – sort of

The Stan Kenton band was another of the Old Man's favorites, so of course, this carried over to his students. To our good fortune, Kenton's clinics for budding jazz musicians were at their peak in the mid-1970s, including week-long summer workshops at several universities around the country. (The clinics started in 1959 and grew in size and number until Stan's passing 20 years later.) I was able to participate in the workshops at Towson State University in Baltimore in 1975 and 1976, both times playing tenor sax.

My first summer at Towson, I was assigned to a band led by composer/arranger Bob Curnow, who worked us really hard – and we loved it. He put so many charts in front of us that everyone's sight-reading improved dramatically in just a few days. We secretly hoped that he would take us on the road after the workshop ended.

Curnow was not on the faculty for the 1976 summer session at Towson. That year, I played in a band led by Ken Hanna, who was also a great composer/arranger but he didn't push us as hard as Curnow had. Fortunately, there were other opportunities to excel.

Students at the workshops had plenty of quality time with the instructors and the Kenton band members, both in formal training sessions and in casual interaction. For example, I learned a lot from Steve Wilkerson, a protégé of Phil Woods, who held the band's lead alto chair in 1975 and went on to be an impressive solo artist and educator. The following year, the band's 1st tenor saxophonist, Roy Reynolds, spent some of his spare time hanging out with the students – which led to an interesting playing experience for me.

As the students went from one activity to the next, we had our horns out, ready to play, all day long. One afternoon, the Kenton band had a rehearsal and we were allowed to be on the stage, looking over the shoulders of the band members as they played. (Kenton used a circular seating arrangement rather than the standard big band rows.) I was standing behind Reynolds with my tenor sax, and suddenly he turned around and said, "Hey Jim, take my place. I'm going out to have a cigarette." I guess that was my 15 minutes of fame – I played with the Kenton band, for part of a rehearsal.

Later that day, I was making a stop in the lavatory and who steps up to the urinal next to me but Stan Kenton himself. So there I was, exchanging banter with the legendary bandleader as we both relieved our bladders. He didn't ask me to join his band, but it was a memorable experience in its own way.

Everybody's favorite band director

In the mid-1990s, I met another remarkable jazz influencer. I had the privilege of working with Gary Langford, an inspiring teacher, bandleader, and jazz player who is known for ending all of his communications with "Now go practice!"

I went to graduate school at the University of Florida (UF) in 1993 to obtain my Ph.D. in political science. I needed to find some musical activity, but not just to keep my chops in shape. I knew that three years of reading political science journal articles and writing research papers would burn out part of my brain unless I was able to routinely exercise the other part that does the music. I found my mental rejuvenation in the UF Jazz Band.

(Photo credit: Gary Langford)

Robert Gary Langford was the band's director, and he generously allowed me to join the sax section even though I was an older grad student who wasn't a music major. I didn't know anything about Gary at the time, but it turns out he was giving me a break similar to what others had done for him during his Air Force service when he was allowed to sit in with jazz bands at the University of Illinois and Oklahoma City University while stationed nearby.

I didn't want to take a lead or solo book because the younger students deserved that experience, so for the next couple years I played 2nd alto or 2nd tenor as needed. That didn't make it any less fun. Gary worked us hard on challenging material. Whenever he put a new chart in front of us, he never said, "Let's take this slow and try to work it up to tempo later." None of that kid stuff. We charged in at full speed and did our best to keep up! This happened often because Gary loved up-tempo charts.

Gary's stimulating leadership style should come as no surprise to anyone who knows his background. He comes from a musical family and started playing trumpet and piano at an early age. His exposure to jazz began at Bucknell University where he majored in music education. Upon graduating in 1962, he was accepted to the U.S. Air Force Band, but after basic training he was shifted to officer training school leading to an assignment in maintenance. When asked why a musician with no maintenance qualifications was given such an assignment, he says "I guess it was because they both begin with 'M'."

After a tour in Vietnam, Gary left the Air Force and took a band director job at a high school in Oklahoma City. That put him in close proximity to the University of North Texas, and the allure of a new challenge was irresistible. In 1969, he enrolled in a master's degree program in trumpet performance at UNT and played in orchestra, brass quintet, and the One O'Clock Lab Band. He also picked up gigs with a variety of groups, including big bands led by trombonists Sy Zentner and Buddy Morrow, usually joining them for two-week tours during the holidays. During his second year, he worked six nights a week in a club in Dallas. How he found time to complete his graduate studies remains a mystery.

But he did complete the degree in 1971, the same year he landed the job at the University of Florida that would establish his musical leadership over the next 36 years. During his tenure at UF he taught trumpet and directed jazz band, concert band, and marching band. His teaching load included courses in music theory and jazz history. The latter was especially popular, and while I was at the university I saw an example of why that was true. One morning, I met Gary on campus and he said, "You should come to my jazz history class at noon today. It's going to be held in the auditorium. There's going to be something special." Intrigued, I did as he suggested.

Gary didn't deliver the lecture that day to his class and other people he invited. The stage was empty, except for a piano, until the surprise appearance of guest lecturer Harry Connick Jr., who happened to be performing in the area. We were treated to stories of how Connick's singing and piano playing evolved. He played examples of tunes and styles that influenced him along the way. This was far superior to watching a YouTube video (which didn't exist at that time). It also demonstrated the clout that Professor Langford had with the artists who were actively making jazz history.

That wasn't the only example of Gary's connections and how he used them to enhance the learning experience. Big names in jazz shared the stage with his students almost every year. While I was playing in the jazz band, we did performances with trombonist Conrad Herwig and drummer Duffy Jackson. Other guest artists over the years have included trumpeters Clark Terry, Bobby Shew, and Wayne Bergeron; saxophonists Don Menza, Chris Vadala, and Ed Calle; trombonist Bill Watrous; drummer Louie Bellson; and singer Joe Williams.

A high point came in 1998 when the UF Jazz Band was invited to perform at the Montreux Jazz Festival in Switzerland. That was two years after I had left the band, prompting me to express my mock outrage that Gary hadn't scheduled this trip a couple of years earlier. He assured me that the bad timing was my fault, not his.

For more than a decade, until his retirement in 2007, Gary was the Assistant Director of UF's school of music. His efforts have earned him a long list of university, state, regional, and national awards for teaching, directing, and expanding the appreciation of music in its various forms. Many of his former students, particularly jazz band alumni, have gone on to careers in academia and in the music industry as composers, arrangers, conductors, and players. And many of them continue to follow him on social media.

As professor emeritus, Gary hasn't been resting on his laurels. He has directed bands for players and listeners of all ages at the local and state level in Florida, including youth orchestras, community concert bands, and the EOS (Every Other Sunday) Big Band. Occasionally, he finds time to play at local jazz clubs.

In addition to the generations of musicians he inspired, Gary also leaves a legacy of recordings with the UF Jazz Band. (See the sample list at the end of this chapter.) Some are concert performances and some were done in studios, but all demonstrate remarkable professionalism.

Shaping the future

There's an old saying that asserts: "Those who can, do; those who can't, teach." I've observed this unfair generalization being applied in many disciplines, including music. As the examples in this chapter show – indeed, as all of the profiles in this book demonstrate – there are many gifted professionals who can *and* do *and* teach. That's why jazz has survived for over a century despite episodes of derision and competition from other musical genres. The people who dedicate their careers to jazz follow a different old saying: "I touch the future – I teach."

Reference

Jim Anastasi oral history video clip
(https://www.namm.org/library/oral-history/jim-anastasi)

Discography

Selected albums by the University of Florida Jazz Band under the direction of Gary Langford
- 1983   Live 1983 (Guest soloist Bobby Shew)
- 1984   Celebration `84 (Guest soloists Louie Bellson and Joe Williams)
- 1992   Festival de Ritmo (Guest soloist Chris Vadala)
- 1995   It Might As Well Be Swing
- 1998   Montreux Bound
- 2007   University of Florida Jazz Band (Guest soloists Ed Calle, Bill Prince, and Terry Moo)

Chapter 6

Jazz Futures

The artists profiled in previous chapters are great musicians who influenced the way many jazz enthusiasts play and think about their music. They deserve more recognition for all they've done in their careers. But they also have something else in common: their focus on the future. They keep their music fresh and share their knowledge and experience with new generations of players and listeners. They all have concerns about how the genre can survive, grow, and be made available to all interested students and audiences. They and many others like them are the reason that jazz is a living, breathing art form. In that sense, this book is as much about the present and future as it is about the past.

Perceptions of jazz

It's no secret that jazz, which some have called America's Music, is not the most popular style of music in the country of its birth. In 2018, just 1.1 percent of all music sold in the United States was jazz, and its market share has been stuck in the one-to-two percent range for many years. Pop/rock, hip-hop, and country music currently dominate the U.S. music market. New generations of composers and arrangers, not surprisingly, tend to follow the money and pursue these genres rather than jazz, thereby creating a cycle that negatively reinforces the perceived status of jazz in the music market. If people are not hearing and recognizing jazz, they're not likely to ask for more of it.

Some would see this as a sign that jazz is an artifact of the past, slowly but surely fading away. Such misperceptions are understandable among those who didn't grow up with significant exposure to the genre in its various forms. Over the years, many people have told me that they don't like jazz. I ask them what jazz they've heard, and why they don't like it. Every time, they have either no answer or an ill-informed answer because they haven't heard enough to enable a well-considered opinion. They don't like it because they don't know it.

Today's music enthusiasts may have an awareness of jazz shaped by their exposure to the soundtracks of old movies and TV shows. Or they may think they know jazz because they used to listen to so-called "smooth jazz" radio stations that featured pop-influenced easy listening played with jazz instrumentation. Or they may have heard about re-releases of albums by artists who have been deceased for decades, and about the efforts of organizations that preserve the work of these late artists, giving the impression that jazz is history, not the present or the future.

What may not be obvious to many listeners is that crossover jazz is all around them, and has been for some time. For example:

- George Benson became a successful pop vocalist with the song "This Masquerade" in 1976. By that time, he had been a respected jazz guitarist for a decade, and he demonstrated this skill in abundance on his recordings and in concert. In fact, "This Masquerade" was the only vocal on his hit album *Breezin'*.
- Al Jarreau started as a jazz vocalist in the 1960s, and the jazz influence in his later work is unmistakable. He won Grammy awards in the pop, jazz, and R&B male vocal categories. Remarkably, his 1982 album *Breakin' Away* earned him Grammys for both best pop vocal and best jazz vocal. The album included two jazz standards, "Teach Me Tonight" and "Blue Rondo a la Turk."
- Linda Ronstadt, at the height of her singing career, released three albums of American Songbook tunes arranged by Nelson Riddle. The first one, *What's New* in 1983, sold five million copies worldwide and earned a Grammy nomination. Among the notable jazz musicians in the orchestra were tenor saxophonists Plas Johnson and Bob Cooper and bassist Ray Brown.
- Lady Gaga and Tony Bennett are two singers you never would have expected to see onstage together prior to their meeting in 2011. They began recording and performing together because Bennett saw Gaga — two generations his junior and aiming her songs at a

completely different audience – as a natural-born jazz singer.
- The 2016 film *La La Land* proved that movie musicals can still be successful, and it won the Academy Award for best original score. The screenplay as well as the score featured jazz; a key aspect of the story focused on present-day jazz culture.
- Jazz pianist, composer, and singer Jon Batiste has received a slew of awards in recent years, including five Grammys in 2022, one of which was for best album. This followed numerous awards (including an Oscar) in 2020, shared with two other composers, for his work on the score of the animated film *Soul*, in which the main character is a jazz pianist.

These and other examples seem to signal a merging of jazz with pop music as a result of increasingly frequent crossover opportunities. This can provide a steady diet of jazz to large and diverse audiences, whether they realize it or not. It may come in the form of a hit song, a movie score, or a TV commercial, and there's no warning label on it saying "You are now listening to jazz." As a result, music sales figures for recordings specifically labeled jazz don't tell the whole story of its place in American culture. As the examples above suggest, coexistence with other genres seems to be paying off – at least for singers and rhythm instrument players.

More than just the backup band

The evolution in popular musical tastes since the 1940s included a gradual loss of audiences' ability to identify with instrumentalists. In the popular music of the 1930s and 40s, Benny Goodman, Tommy Dorsey, Glenn Miller, and other soloist/bandleaders were the stars, while vocalists like Frank Sinatra and Peggy Lee were added attractions who only sang a few tunes at each performance. That turned around quickly, driven by two significant occurrences: World War II disrupted the careers of working musicians across the country; and at the same time, the musicians union staged a strike known as the Recording Ban (1942-44) that prevented instrumentalists (but not vocalists) from making new recordings. This prompted singers to record songs using unaccompanied vocal harmonies, and allowed record companies to re-release old recordings with new labels showing the singers as the headliners (for example, Frank Sinatra instead of Tommy Dorsey). By the time the war and the Recording Ban ended, vocalists had become the new stars, and the instrumentalists increasingly were seen as merely their backup. This shift in roles has remained in place ever since, and the disparity between vocalist celebrities and their band members tends to increase as star power and colorful personalities overshadow the music itself.

An argument could be made that full appreciation of jazz requires equal recognition of both vocalists and instrumentalists for their talent and their body of work. This is not the default situation in most types of modern popular music, where singers can be American Idols but instrumentalists can't. Of course, there have been some "rock stars" who are recognized for their playing rather than their singing, like guitarists Eric Clapton and Eddie Van Halen. But such individuals have been rare and usually play rhythm instruments. They managed to inspire a video game that was popular for a while called Guitar Hero. But I'm still waiting for Saxophone Hero.

Renewed recognition of the instrumentalist is one of the prerequisites for stimulating popular appreciation for today's jazz music. There are signs that we may be striking a new balance that will mitigate the long-running vocalist bias. I certainly hope we've moved beyond the perplexing experience I had at a concert in 1977. The venue was on a university campus, so the audience was relatively young. Chuck Mangione, at the height of his popularity, was performing to a full house with his quartet plus a ten-piece brass and percussion ensemble. By intermission, I knew that this would be one of the most memorable concerts I'd ever attend. The soloists were hot and the brass arrangements were beautiful. The second half of the concert began with a medley from a movie score Mangione had recently written for *The Children of Sanchez.* The piece opened with a rubato introduction in which the bass player sang the lyrics of the title song. As soon as this started, a guy sitting behind me said, in an exasperated voice, "Oh, thank God, finally – a vocal." I didn't know whether to pity him or smack some sense into him. I did neither – I just wondered how many in the crowd that night felt the same way, and failed to share in the extraordinary concert experience I was having.

Almost everyone has a voice, so they can enjoy singing whether or not they have exceptional vocal talent. This enables people to identify with vocalists more readily than with instrumentalists. The extra hardware and training needed to play an instrument can be a mystery to those unfamiliar with it – until they discover new sounds that they like.

In the 1960s, some pop music audiences still liked tunes featuring horns, as demonstrated, for example, by the success of trumpeters Al Hirt and Herb Alpert, and the Latin-style recordings of tenor saxophonist Stan Getz. They were followed by the prominent use of horns in rock groups such as Blood, Sweat & Tears and Chicago. But then the disco era of the 1970s pushed horn sections into the background, and the instrumental solos in pop music tended to go to guitar or keyboard. Pop music listeners didn't have many opportunities to hear beautiful and thrilling displays of musicianship from horn players that would prompt them to think, "Hey, I really like that. Where can I find more?"

Slowly, over a period of decades, instrumental music has been making a comeback. In part, this has been driven by the extraordinary popularity of movie scores by John Williams, Hans Zimmer, Quincy Jones, Danny Elfman, and others. One of the biggest turning points was the 1981 release of *Chariots of Fire*, scored by Vangelis, although the beneficiary was electronic music, to the detriment of horns and strings. In any case, movie music was winning high-visibility awards and contributing to greater appreciation of instrumental offerings.

By the 1990s and beyond, a few horn players found success on the pop music charts, such as saxophonist Kenny G and trumpeter Chris Botti. This was not without its pitfalls. Kenny G in particular was criticized for selling out as a jazz artist and for delivering music that didn't challenge him or his audience. Whether one thinks these criticisms are fair or not, it is undeniable that Kenny G and others like him have exposed audiences to jazz-inspired sounds that could lead to greater acceptance of instrumental music in pop culture, to the benefit of jazz musicians.

The efforts of jazz musicians to join the hit parade have been evident for a long time. For example, many jazz artists in the 1960s tried to expand their audience by recording albums displaying their mellow side. Even power trumpeter Maynard Ferguson recorded an easy listening album (*The Ballad Style of Maynard Ferguson*, 1969). The surprising extent of this phenomenon should be evident by the fact that I just used "Maynard Ferguson" and "easy listening" in the same sentence.

Jazz musicians have a long heritage, and as the profiles in this book demonstrate, they'll do their part to secure the future of the genre. Jazz is not in danger of becoming a lost art thanks to players' dedication and two additional factors: the extensive international community of jazz fans, and the spectacular growth of jazz education.

World music

It used to be fashionable to say that America is a melting pot of ethnicities and cultures. Jazz is a product of that environment, a musical stew with ingredients from Africa, Europe, Latin America, and many places on the map of the United States. It's extraordinarily versatile, so there's something for every race, gender, and age group.

American audiences may be surprised to learn that jazz enjoys popularity in many parts of the world. Since 2011, the United Nations Educational, Scientific, and Cultural Organization (UNESCO) has recognized April 30 as International Jazz Day, celebrated in 2022 with 772 events in 132 countries. Annual jazz festivals are held in about 60 countries. Canada, with a population just 11 percent of the size of the United States, is among the most active countries with as many as 20 annual festivals coast-to-coast. There are five European countries that hold at least 10 festivals per year. (For comparison, the United States has about 80 annual jazz festivals.)

Australia and several Asian countries also have energetic jazz communities.

My experiences on multiple trips to Taiwan provide an example. During a visit in 2008, I shopped at a high-rise department store in downtown Taipei that offered mostly books, music, and videos. I was surprised and pleased to find a large wall display devoted to jazz recordings, in greater abundance and variety than you'll find in most places in the United States. Moving on to the magazine section, there were no less than five different English-language jazz magazines. On another trip in 2015, I got an opportunity to try out an assortment of saxophones at the Lien Cheng Saxophone Company in Taichung, where they told me that saxes had become an extraordinarily popular instrument for Taiwan's music students. I took that as a good omen for jazz awareness because I doubt that the students are using saxes to play traditional Chinese music or European classics. These and other episodes made me wonder when American students would rediscover the homegrown treasure that is jazz.

Jazz jocks

It's possible that the rediscovery has already started. There's more jazz in U.S. schools today than ever before. There may even be places where the students who play jazz are the cool kids. It certainly wasn't like that when I was in school.

I began studying music when I got to high school in 1968, when jazz-oriented student groups typically were called "dance band" or "stage band." Many academic institutions considered jazz to be indecent and somehow detrimental to the proper execution of more respectable forms of music like classical. Our "jazz" repertoire mostly consisted of simple arrangements of old standards, and occasionally we played for dances in addition to appearing in the school band concerts. There was no improvisation – we just tried our best to make the written solos sound good.

Band members were not seen as the cool kids at my all-boys college prep high school, where an assortment of sports were the overriding focus of campus life. The football and basketball teams frequently brought home championship trophies, and other sports did well too. Those of us in the band were considered nerds by the sports jocks. (Actually, "nerd" wasn't a popular expression in those days – they tended to use a variety of other derogatory terms.) They saw us as losers who didn't have the right stuff. In their eyes, the only reason to join the band was because you were incapable of doing sports. My retort to them was: "Thirty years from now, I'll still be playing music, and I'll be far better at it than I am now. Can you say the same about football?"

The jocks didn't accept my logic, but it turns out I was right. It's now *50 years* since I finished high school, and I'm still playing an assortment of instruments – much better than I did back then. I bet the jocks from the class of 1972 quit playing team sports decades ago. They have to be content with watching it on TV as they consume unhealthy quantities of beer and snacks.

Plenty has changed in the past half-century for both sports and music. When I was in school, we heard of a foreign game called soccer that looked like hockey played outdoors and without the ice. But nobody played it or watched it. Today, the game is a hit with kids of all ages, there are men's and women's professional soccer leagues, and lots of Americans tune in to telecasts of U.S. and international teams in competition. Can jazz music experience a similar renaissance?

Cool curricula

Jazz programs in U.S. schools have demonstrated impressive growth in their number and quality. The first university jazz studies program was at North Texas in the late 1940s, and 20 years later there were still only a handful of universities with similar offerings. But today, jazz studies can be found at well over 200 U.S. colleges and universities. High school and middle school programs have grown as well, and the summer 2022 jazz camp schedule offered students immersive experiences at 86 locations across the country.

As in sports, the discipline that music students learn will benefit them for years to come, whether or not they become career musicians. The aim is to design stimulating and well-resourced programs to get kids' attention early and keep them interested. They want something that's fun, challenging, and allows them to stand out among their peers. So it's encouraging to see that improvisation is now taught as early as middle school, instead of waiting until college to introduce it, as in olden times (i.e., when I was in school).

Characteristics such as early exposure, openness, persistence, and casting a wide net are desirable in education and training programs in many disciplines. In my career, I heard plenty of discussion about STEM education – science, technology, engineering, and math. The same lessons apply in music: for example, women and minorities can contribute as much as anyone to the profession if they have opportunities and role models. Both jazz and STEM need to develop a cadre of professionals that cultivates talent wherever it can be found, and an even larger population of non-professionals who understand and appreciate the significance of what's at stake (informed citizens for STEM; informed audiences for jazz).

Just like sports, music has considerable allure even though it requires regular training and practice, incurs costs, and doesn't always pay for itself in earnings. Every kid has a desire to seek out a superpower, and music is a great choice. Your instrument can be your Iron Man suit. If a person is willing to put in the time and effort, they will eventually become one with the instrument. If they find good venues to exercise their skills, they can experience a natural high, just like what's possible in sports. But unlike sports, this hands-on activity can last a lifetime, its intellectual and emotional intensity growing across decades. Not many of life's callings can do that.

A coming resurgence?

Attempts to describe jazz typically identify its primary attributes as improvisation and rhythmic syncopation. But looking at it from an empirical rather than structural perspective, the elements of jazz also include freedom and diversity – characteristics perceived in unique ways by each participant that go beyond the music printed on a page or heard at a performance. Those characteristics are desperately needed today, and jazz can be a valuable medium for sharing them.

As in other areas of human experience, the future is what we make it. The role models highlighted in this book have risen to that challenge and have taught us that jazz has strengths that are leading it to a more prominent and productive future with its cultural relevance undiminished. Their persistent efforts increase the probability that jazz music has many good years ahead, possibly surpassing those that have already passed.

References

DeVeaux, Scott. "Bebop and the Recording Industry: The 1942 AFM Recording Ban Reconsidered," *Journal of the American Musicological Society*, Vol. 41, No. 1 (Spring, 1988), pp. 126-165 (http://www.jstor.org/stable/831753?origin=JSTOR-pdf).

Downbeat Magazine, "Where to Study Jazz in 2022," Vol. 88, No. 10, October 2021 (https://downbeat.com/magazine/2021-10)

Downbeat Magazine, "2022 Summer Jazz Camp Guide," Vol. 89, No. 3, March 2022 (https://downbeat.com/magazine/2022-03)

Downbeat Magazine, "2022 Jazz Festival Guide," Vol. 89, No. 5, May 2022 (https://downbeat.com/magazine/2022-05)

International Jazz Day (https://jazzday.com)

Jazz Festivals Canada (https://www.jazzfestivalscanada.ca)

JazzInAmerica.org, "The Rise of Formal Jazz Education" (https://www.jazzinamerica.org/jazzresources/jazzeducation/page/163)

National Jazz Festival (https://www.nationaljazzfestival.org)

Statista: Share of total music album consumption in the United States in 2018, by genre (https://www.statista.com/statistics/310746/share-music-album-sales-us-genre/)

Universities.com, "Best Jazz/Jazz Studies colleges in the U.S. for 2022" lists 76 programs (https://www.universities.com/programs/jazz-jazz-studies-degrees)

About the author

James A. Vedda is a retired technology policy analyst who spent most of his career with government contractors in the Washington, D.C. area researching civil, commercial, and national security space issues. He has a Ph.D. in political science, a master's degree in science and technology policy, and a bachelor's degree in business administration. Previously, Jim was an associate professor in the Department of Space Studies at the University of North Dakota, where he taught courses on civil, commercial, and military space policy to undergraduate and graduate students. He was one of the founding members of the department.

Jim has been playing saxophones, flute, and clarinet since high school, and has been performing in a variety of ensembles since then. Currently, he plays baritone sax with two jazz ensembles in the Washington, DC area. He also publishes jazz ensemble arrangements of his original compositions and jazz standards.

Made in the USA
Coppell, TX
27 November 2022